STRETCH YOUR SOUL

A Gift For:

_____

From:

_____

Training Table: 10 For 10
© The Core Media Group, Inc., 2010

Published in association with Sports Spectrum Publishing.

The Core Media Group, Inc., titles may be purchased in bulk for educational, business, fund-raising, or sales promotional use. For information, please email new@sportsspectrum.com

Visit our websites: www.thecoremediagroup.com / www.sportsspectrum.com

Credits
Project Manager: Ryan J. DiNunzio
Copy Editor: Brett Honeycutt
Book and Cover Design: Ryan J. DiNunzio

ISBN: 978-0-9844670-1-3

Printed in the United States of America

SPORTS DEVOTIONALS FOR THE SEASONS WITHIN THE SEASON

Po Box 2037, Indian Trail, NC 28079

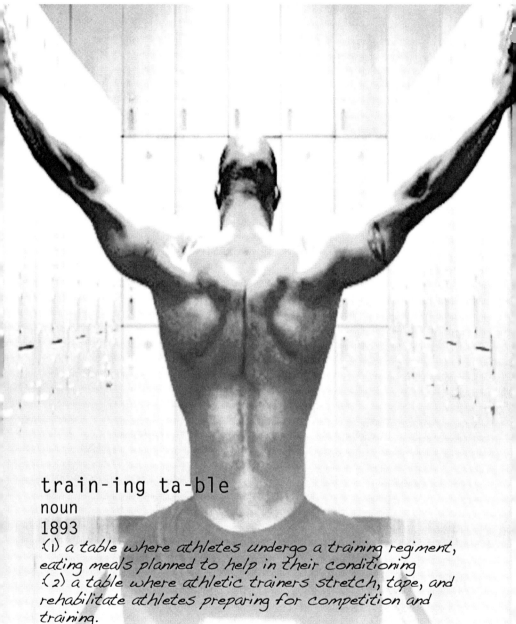

train-ing ta-ble
noun
1893
(1) a table where athletes undergo a training regiment, eating meals planned to help in their conditioning
(2) a table where athletic trainers stretch, tape, and rehabilitate athletes preparing for competition and training.

The Core Media Group, Inc., and *Sports Spectrum* magazine present their own version of the training table, a place where someone can indulge in the Bread of Life while God stretches their soul, rehabilitates old injuries and prepares the soul for daily spiritual battles.

CONTENTS

Introduction VII

THE SEASONS

INDIVIDUAL MEETINGS 1
Character, Accountability, Discipline

TEAM MEETINGS 13
Teamwork, Unity

GOAL SETTING 25
Purpose, Direction, Responsibility

PRESEASON 37
Preparation, Readiness

REGULAR SEASON 49
Servanthood, Sacrifice, Humility

THE TRAINING ROOM 61
Perseverance, Patience, Pain

THE TRAINING GROUND 73
Work Ethic, Passion, Commitment

PLAYOFFS 85
Leadership, God's Authority

THE CHAMPIONSHIP 97
Excellence, Perfection

AWARDS BANQUET 109
God's... Grace, Truth, Love

Scripture Index 121
Training Table Contributors 123

" ...praying at all times in the Spirit, with all prayer and supplication. To that end keep alert with all perseverance..."

Ephesians 6:18 (ESV)

INTRODUCTION

The sporting calendar never ends, does it? No matter what the time of year, there is either one or more sports seasons beginning or ending. This does not provide a break for sports fans, there really is not an off-season. Athletes, coaches, and fans always find themselves either in the preseason, regular season, playoffs, or draft season, etc. There is never an end, the calendar is constantly changing.

Our lives as Christians reflects this as well. We never get a break, we are always in season. Like the professional leagues, our season has shorter seasons within it - preseason, playoffs, you get the picture. We all know how much work, time, and effort it takes for any team to have a successful season; to be a fruitful follower of Christ is no different. To be at your best you must be focused and maintain strong habits. Christ demonstrated this greater than anyone.

As He walked through the seasons within His season, He provided great truths for us to follow. Jesus, being the Word of God, knew all of scripture and was constantly in prayer. For us to know and be in the Word of God, we must read it.

Training Table: 10 For 10 - Sports Devotionals for the Season Within the Season, provides you an opportunity to abide in God's Word. Whether you are an athlete, coach, or fan, the biblical principles you will find here are applicable to further your walk with Jesus as you find yourself in different seasons within the season of life.

No matter where you may be - in individual meetings doing some deep reflection, grinding through the playoffs, or even preparing for the awards banquet - there are lessons to be learned, and encouraging words to be read.

May God bless you in your season. May you live in His love. May you be a beacon of light pointing to Christ on and off the fields of play. Your season has already started - evaluate where you are, and get to it!

" Watch your thoughts, for they
become words. Watch your words,
for they become actions. Watch
your actions, for they become habits.
Watch your habits, for they become
character. Watch your character, for
it becomes your destiny."

        - Anonymous

" But those that were sown on the
good soil are the ones who hear
the word and accept it and bear
fruit, thirtyfold and sixtyfold and a
hundredfold."

        - Mark 4:20

CHARACTER, ACCOUNTABILITY, DISCIPLINE

Our faith, our walk with Christ, is a personal journey. It is crucial for followers of Christ to behave in a manner that is above reproach, and which presents the gospel in an exemplary manner. To do so we must be men and women of the highest CHARACTER, we are to be ACCOUNTABLE for all of our actions, and we need to be DISCIPLINED in the love of Christ. Before any season, athletes have **individual meetings** with their coach for self-evaluation and growth.

ABOVE THE RIM

" ...that you may be blameless and innocent, children of God without blemish in the midst of a crooked and twisted generation, among whom you shine as lights in the world..."

PHILIPPIANS 2:15 (ESV)

This is a hard thing for me write about; it takes a great deal of vulnerability, so instead of using my own life as an example, I will point to some sports news. During the Winter of 2009. The sporting world was rocked by revelations of inappropriate behaviors by two men, Tiger Woods and Ben Roethlisberger. By no means am I judging these men, that is for God; I just want to use them in this illustration. These men have made some mistakes; for the rest of their lives they will continue to be under great scrutiny and will need to live their lives way "Above the Rim" in an area where none of their actions can be questioned.

The lesson to be learned in this: as Christians we are already under heavy scrutiny for our beliefs, and for us to be successful in sharing the gospel, we too must live "Above the Rim," an area that cannot be touched. By this I mean we are called to build good reputations by being vulnerable with others and developing interpersonal relationships with everyone we continually interact with. To do this, stay clear of gossip, keep out of questionable situations, and ask yourself this, "If Christ returned right now, would I want Him to find me at this moment?" Today, be consistent, let your actions and words be in line with scripture and your calling from God.

— RYAN J. DINUNZIO

Are you transparent; are your actions in line with your character? _____

_____

_____

_____

_____

_____

_____

_____

_____

_____

_____

_____

_____

YOU'RE NOT ALONE

" But encourage one another daily, as long as it is called Today, so that none of you may be hardened by sin's deceitfulness."

HEBREWS 3:13

Much of the 2010 World Cup discussion revolved around the officiating - specifically here in America where we are accustomed to instant replay, apologies, and explanations. Soccer, however, is different. When the U.S.A. played Slovenia in the World Cup, referee Koman Coulibaly waived off Maurice Edu's goal and didn't explain the call, sending all of America into a state of Sturm and Drang.

In the Associated Press's article "FIFA Unfazed by Criticism of Refs," Jose-Marcia Garcia-Aranda, the head of refereeing for the sport's governing body, was quoted saying, "The duty of the referees is not to explain their decision ... [but to] try to do their best on the field of play. [Otherwise] they are not focused on the game, they are focused on the media."

The more I pondered the questions above, the more I realized that we, too, are soccer referees. Because of the forgiveness, love, confidence, hope, and joy that Christ brings, we have power. Because of the Holy Spirit, there is no limit to what we can do on this earth for God's kingdom. Because of Christ, we have the ability to change the outcome of the game for the better.

We, however, unlike the nature of soccer and its referees, can't do this alone. Because there is so much at stake, we need to surround ourselves with accountability. We are human. We will fail. And we need others to keep us in check.

Surely, we can't do this alone. There is too much at stake.

—STEPHEN COPELAND

Who in your life can you lean on for accountability?_____

_____

_____

_____

_____

_____

_____

_____

_____

_____

_____

_____

_____

THE TRUTH

"Then you will know the truth, and the truth will set you free."

JOHN 8:32

As an NFL agent there are many opportunities to not tell the truth; whether in recruiting a player or talking to team management. I have players call me in many instances and say my agent said this or my agent never followed through or my agent is not being honest with me. You could probably build your business faster by telling people what they want to hear, but the long term effects will be long lasting.

The truth can be very painful to accept sometimes, but the truth will also be a motivation to at least know where you stand. At our firm, US Sports Management, we work very hard on being honest with all of our clients and the teams we work with. There will be times where we could have not told the truth and it may have benefited me and my firm, but I have chosen to tell the truth.

When you have to make a call to a player and tell them what a team thinks about them, it can be uncomfortable for you and the player. When a player is on the way to a workout and the teams ask if he is healthy, but you know he is not 100 percent, it can be an uncomfortable situation. However, at the end of the day, the truth will set you free, and the truth will build bridges to others who will help you get through life. So today, make it a point to tell the truth.

— ROBERT WALKER

Does it take more self-control to speak the truth, or lie? Are you disciplined to speak the truth at all times even though it may be hurtful?

_____

_____

_____

_____

_____

_____

_____

_____

_____

_____

_____

_____

_____

DAILY WALK WITH CHRIST

" So I say, live by the Spirit, and you will not gratify the desires of the sinful nature. For the sinful nature desires what is contrary to the Spirit, and the Spirit what is contrary to the sinful nature. They are in conflict with each other, so that you do not do what you want."

GALATIANS 5:16-17

Everyone wants to win. Winning itself, however, isn't easy. There is conflict, fighting, and in the end, there is a winner and a loser. The team that has more talent and practices the hardest leading up to the game will most likely win.

In Galatians 5:16, Paul talks about another type of conflict: a spiritual conflict. He says that the Spirit and a man's sinful nature are in constant battle with one another. The Spirit urges man to live a righteous life that is pleasing to God while the sinful nature tempts man to live a sinful, pleasure-seeking life that is accepted by the world.

In the end, the Spirit is the ultimate winner. It has more talent and power than the sinful nature; but strangely, it doesn't always win. That's because Christians don't always "live by the Spirit" as Paul urges the Galatians to do in 5:16.

The most talented team, for example, can still lose – especially if they don't practice in a winning manner. In the Holy Spirit, Christians have the most powerful, influential, and unexplainable tool this world has ever known. But sometimes, it isn't effective because of the effort on our end. We don't always practice or live by the Spirit.

To combat our sinful desire, Christians must "live by the Spirit" on a daily, hourly, and minutely basis. That means engaging in steadfast prayer, delving into scripture, and living in a Christ-honoring manner. By daily living in a winning manner, the most talented team cannot lose.

— STEPHEN COPELAND

*Does your daily life contain the Spirit? Does He guide you?*_____

_____

_____

_____

_____

_____

_____

_____

ASHAMED?

"Therefore, knowing the fear of the lord, we persuade others. But what we are is known to God, and I hope it is known also to your conscience."

II CORINTHIANS 5:11

Over the past 20 years, professional athletes have achieved high-profile status in our society. The public spotlight and the high place in society typically come to players who have great success in their sports. The public always wants to know more about first-class performers. What athletes do on the field is seen, respected, and adored by thousands if not millions. We as fans really only see game time performances; we aren't with the players on a daily basis seeing what they do to reach such a high level.

Recently, more and more athletes are being caught and accused of cheating. Unless an athlete is humble enough to be honest, we really never know. It is becoming far too common for athletes to deceive the fans by cheating their way to our adoration; however, God knows.

It is easy for followers of Christ to put on "great performances" in our community by establishing "Christ-centered relationships." Yet, at times we deceive those relationships when we are called to love. Some of the Churches best "performers" have deceived us in the past; it is amazing what fame and fortune can lead people to do. But we must be careful, for we can fall prey to "faking it" as well. Not only does God see what we do in our private time, but also He sees deeper and looks directly into our hearts. Would you be ashamed for God to look into your heart today?

— RYAN J. DINUNZIO

How is your heart being shaped? _____

_____

_____

_____

_____

_____

_____

_____

_____

_____

ACCOUNTABILITY

"Two are better than one because they have a good return for their labor. For if either of them falls, the one will lift up his companion. But woe to the one who falls when there is not another to lift him up."

ECCLESIASTES 4:9-10

One of the secrets to reaching goals is to effectively partner with someone to help you reach your goals. This can be a mentor, a friend to exercise with, or a personal trainer to make sure you exercise each week.

As we have designed fitness routines for executives and many athletes through the years, the one reason many of them reach their goals is that we hold them accountable by weekly measurements. For weight loss, it is as simple as stepping on the scales and then adjusting our actions for the week based on the outcome. For football players trying to improve their 40-yard dash times, it is videoing their running form and weekly clocking their times so we can make adjustments in their training.

Acknowledging that we need assistance is not a flaw, but a sign of wisdom as long as we realize we have to do the work. A partner can hold us accountable and keep a temporary setback from becoming a permanent failure.

Seek assistance to achieve accountability and you'll be on your way to achieve your goals.

— ALAN TYSON

Do you find it difficult to seek help? _____

_____

_____

_____

_____

_____

_____

_____

_____

_____

_____

_____

_____

_____

IN THE ZONE

" But the fruit of the Spirit is love, joy, peace, patience, kindness, goodness, faithfulness, gentleness, self-control..."

GALATIANS 5:22-23

On May 7, 1995, The Indiana Pacers and the New York Knicks met for Game 1 of the NBA Eastern Conference semifinals. With 20 seconds remaining, the Knicks held a fairly comfortable six point lead. Then, something amazing happened. With 18.7 seconds remaining and the Pacers trailing by six points, Reggie Miller made a three-point shot, stole the inbounds pass from Greg Anthony, dribbled back to the three-point arc and tied the game with a second three-pointer, stunning the Knicks bench and their fans. On the ensuing possession, Knicks guard John Starks was fouled but missed both free throws. Patrick Ewing managed to rebound the second miss, but his shot rattled out. Miller rebounded the ball, was fouled, and made both free throws. Trailing by two points, the New York Knicks had one last chance to tie or win the game, but failed to get a shot off, giving Miller and the Pacers a stunning 107-105 victory. Reggie Miller had scored 8 points in 8.9 seconds. There is no doubt, Reggie Miller was "in the zone" that day!

We often talk about athletes being "in the zone," but have you ever experienced this in your life? When you are living life "in the zone" all the parts of your life just seem to click. Paul challenges us in Galatians 5:16 to "walk in the Spirit." He goes on to indicate that if we walk in the Spirit we will experience the fruits of the Spirit in our lives. If we will discipline ourselves to walk in the Spirit, we will begin to portray the fruits of the Spirit listed in Galatians 5:22-23, and then we will begin to experience what it means to live our lives "in the zone"!

— TODD GREEN

An athlete needs solid mental preparation to get in the zone. What do you do to get in the zone?

_____

_____

_____

_____

_____

_____

_____

_____

_____

ENCOURAGING WORDS

"The men were sent off and went down to Antioch, where they gathered the church together and delivered the letter. The people read it and were glad for its encouraging message. Judas and Silas, who themselves were prophets, said much to encourage and strengthen the brothers."

ACTS 15:30-32

Major League Baseball players Josh Hamilton, Michael Young and Mike Sweeney all seem to share the same sentiment about New York Yankees slugger Mark Teixeira. He works hard, he's a good guy and he's a strong Christian.

"I really didn't know he was a Christian until I got around him and started talking to him," says Hamilton. "You can just tell when you talk to somebody, you really can. The Holy Spirit just kind of draws you and lets you know, 'Hey, this guy is one of us.' It's always good to have that comfort, that encouragement from guys around the league."

Is your life an encouragement to others? Can they see Christ in your actions, words and deeds? If not, ask God to help you live a life pleasing to Him so that He can be known by believers, and also by a lost and dying world desperate for Him. If your life is pleasing to God, be encouraged that He is manifesting Himself through you to people, believers and non-believers, who are desperate to see someone who is real.

— BRETT HONEYCUTT

Does your life lead others to know you are a follower of Christ? _____

_____

_____

_____

_____

_____

_____

_____

_____

_____

_____

_____

9

MAN IN THE MIRROR

" Each one test his own actions. Then he can take pride in himself, without comparing himself to somebody else, for each one should carry his own load."

GALATIANS 6:4 (ESV)

As a professional soccer player for six years I fell into many traps as I navigated my way through my career. But one trap I fell into was one that caught me because of habits I learned early in my life. As athletes we often measure ourselves by comparing ourselves to others. In all of athletics success is measured by comparison—records, statistics, salaries, etc. the list goes on and on.

Early in my career, I found myself comparing me to my other teammates; at the age of 21-22 during my first and second seasons out of college measuring myself against men more than 6 years my senior who had played professionally for several years. Every time I looked at the comparisons I kept falling short. Sure it drove me to succeed and push myself to get better, but the comparisons never allowed me to be joyful in who I was or where I was; I always was unsatisfied. I couldn't find joy. Then one day, sharing this with a teammate he simply said to me, "Ryan, comparison smothers joy." Wow! He explained that I only need to look at myself and measure my growth against where I started not against anyone else. The more I learned to do this, the more joy I experienced, and the more success I experienced in my career.

As followers of Christ, it is very easy to find ourselves comparing who we are to those we see at Church and others in our lives; this often leaves us unsatisfied and joyless in Christ. Paul teaches us that we must only look and measure who we are and are becoming against who we were and where we started. Don't let your joy in Christ be smothered by comparison. There is an ancient proverb that echoes my teammate's word, "There is nothing noble about being superior to some other man. The true nobility is being superior to your previous self."

— RYAN J. DINUNZIO

Are you being a thief of joy in your life or that of anyone else? _____

_____

_____

_____

_____

_____

_____

_____

_____

KEEP YOUR EYE ON THE BALL!

"Your eye is the lamp to your body. When your eyes are good, your whole body also is full of light. But when they are bad, your body also is full of darkness."

LUKE 11:34

Many athletes are known for their great eyes. Joe Mauer, the great young catcher for the Minnesota Twins, became the first catcher in the major leagues to win a batting title. That number is now three and counting. He obviously has a great eye as a hitter. The Lord is looking for all men to have eyes dedicated and disciplined for Him. Men of all ages today are being hit from every angle by sexual images. Because of this, it is critical for us to have male fellowship and accountability partners.

Bill McCartney, the founder of Promise Keepers, spoke of the importance of men meeting in small groups. The small gatherings allowed the men to share their sin struggles and temptations with each other. It was proven that a large group inhibited the men from sharing openly. I was a member of a small group and we expressed ourselves easily and had great success in fighting temptation. We all were given a small "check point" card that we would cover each week. The seventh and final question on the card was; "Have you just lied to me?"

One of the greatest benefits of athletic participation involves personal discipline. This practice must include our spiritual life or we will fall victim to temptation. My friend Zig Ziglar once said; "If you do not stand for something, you will fall for anything!" As coaches, athletes and Christians, we must commit to seeking God first in all things and know that He will give us the strength that is needed in this troubled world.

— JONATHAN CORRAO

For what do you stand? _____

_____

_____

_____

_____

_____

_____

_____

_____

_____

_____

_____

"Coming together is a beginning. Keeping together is progress. Working together is success."

— Henry Ford

"Finally, all of you, have unity of mind, sympathy, brotherly love, a tender heart, and a humble mind."

— I Peter 3:8 (ESV)

team meetings

We are the body of Christ. We are to operate as one. All throughout the season there are **team meetings,** to learn, assess, and communicate. TEAMWORK is critical to success as an athlete and as an individual. In Jesus' ministry no one disciple worked independently, they worked together as a team. It was UNITY that spurred the growth of the Church. It was unity that supported the growth of followers of Christ.

A HOUSE DIVIDED

" And Jesus knew their thoughts, and said unto them, Every kingdom divided against itself is brought to desolation; and every city or house divided against itself shall not stand" Matthew 12:25 (KJV)

MATTHEW 12:25 (KJV)

No, the above phrase isn't talking about a North Carolina and Duke fan living together. Instead, I'm talking about 2009-10 University of North Carolina men's basketball team, which seemed to have a divided house as the Tar Heels struggled through the regular season.

There were many reasons that players, coaches, and fans came up with to try and explain what went on with the Tar Heels. One player, Deon Thompson, mentioned a possible crack between the veterans and the new kids, and teammate Marcus Ginyard said they didn't play as a team. Whatever the reason, it was evident that they didn't play together.

When we try to do life in similar ways, we miss out on helping and encouraging others and therefore miss out on the blessings God has for us and the opportunity to build into people's lives. When we work together as a team, we can accomplish so much more.

The acronym for Team is: Together, Everyone Achieves More.

Are we playing the game of life individually, or as a team?

— JASON BELCHER

What examples in life prove to you that teamwork always yields a greater reward? _____

_____

_____

_____

_____

_____

_____

_____

_____

_____

_____

PLAY YOUR POSITION

" Just as each of us has one body with many members, and these members do not all have the same function, so in Christ we who are many form one body, and each member belongs to all the others. We have different gifts, according to the grace given us."

ROMANS 12:4-6a

The foundation of every good team is built upon the combined talents and skills of the players on the field and coaches on the sidelines. Typically, the best teams have a vast array of talented individuals at multiple positions who each contribute to the performance of the team. Everyone specializes in something different, and how those individual pieces comprise the bigger puzzle will ultimately determine how successful a team will be in the long run.

In football, linemen typically aren't asked to run deep routes and make fingertip catches. Likewise, wide receivers don't always make the best blockers against blitzing linebackers. In soccer, goalkeepers are asked to perform tasks that most offensive-minded players haven't practiced in years. Pitchers have a different job than a team's best sluggers in baseball. Coaches call the shots and guarantee that the team is prepared, both mentally and physically. Trainers and fans play a specific role as well in a team's success. In the end, the sum of the "parts" (the individual positions and roles on a team) ultimately determines how solid the "whole" (the team) will be.

The same principle applies to the body of believers. God has called us to different roles by blessing us with individual talents, gifts, and responsibilities. For some, those gifts may be leadership or teaching. For others, it may be encouragement or charity. Regardless, God expects us to use those gifts that He has given toward the betterment of others, and to the success of His team.

How are you playing your "position" in life? Is there something that you are (or are not) doing that might be holding "the team" back from spreading God's love to those who don't know Him?

— COREY THOMPSON

How do you determine your role? _____

_____

_____

_____

_____

_____

_____

TEAM SUCCESS

" ...who gave himself for us to redeem us from all lawlessness and to purify for himself a people for his own possession who are zealous for good works."

TITUS 2:14 (ESV)

No matter what the sport or level, you always hear pundits, analysts, experts, coaches, you name it, emphasizing the importance of unity for success. Think about the last five championship games you watched, or championship teams you read about; one of the first things mentioned is how great the team chemistry was and how unified they were. It is true that you never see a team of dysfunction accomplish anything, just look at the Raiders (sorry Oakland fans).

The same is true about our workplaces, and more importantly the church, the body of Christ. If we are all one Church and are called to reclaim the Kingdom for God, why do we struggle? Is it the gossiping or the hypocritical attitudes and behavior? I don't know.

What I do know is that we must be doing more to unify the church. I find it a struggle each day when interacting with some people in my church, but I pray to God for patience and understanding. Because if I don't, I won't love that individual where they are, and I will be ruining our church chemistry. I have to check my heart constantly.

Think today about where you may be hurting team unity; is it your office or your church? What can you do to improve unity and foster success? Pray, because God will answer.

— RYAN J. DINUNZIO

How did Christ foster teamwork? _____

_____

_____

_____

_____

_____

_____

_____

_____

_____

_____

_____

_____

AT ODDS

" How good and pleasant it is
when God's people live together in unity!
It is like precious oil poured on the head,
running down on the beard, "
PSALM 133:1-2

Have you ever had a teammate that became angry easily and was always trying to start fights? Maybe a couple of players who were really good friends and didn't include everyone else on the team? As a player, that can be really frustrating. It hurts teamwork, and can cause lots of problems over a season. I have been on teams like that, but I have also been on teams where everyone was really good friends and everyone got along really well. That team was so much more fun to play on, and we won more games as well.

In Psalm 133, David talks about God's people living together in unity. As Christians, we have to remember that other Christians are our brothers and sisters in Christ. We work together for the same goal of glorifying God. If Christians are always fighting, or don't get along with each other, God is not pleased with that, and we become a bad testimony to the world. Do we work on getting along with everyone, or are we stuck in our own circles more worried about ourselves than others?

—NATHAN WADE

What are the negatives of unity? What are the positives? _____

_____

_____

_____

_____

_____

_____

_____

_____

_____

_____

_____

_____

_____

TEAM UNITY DEFINED

" Therefore if there is any consolation in Christ, if any comfort of love, if any fellowship of the Spirit, if any affection and mercy, 2 fulfill my joy by being like-minded, having the same love, being of one accord, of one mind. Let nothing be done through selfish ambition or conceit, but in lowliness of mind let each esteem others better than himself. Let each of you look out not only for his own interests, but also for the interests of others."

PHILIPPIANS 2:1-4 (NKJV)

Paul tells us specifically what walking worthy looks like for an athletic team. First, it involves being like-minded, having the same love, and being of one accord, of one mind. Being "likeminded" is being "one-souled" people who are knit together in harmony, having the same desires, passions, and ambitions. Everyone is all on the same page, with the same goals. A team that is truly unified looks the same, acts the same, and can even think the same.

We have all seen teams like this. One player knows exactly what the other player is thinking, and what that player will do in a certain situation. True team unity is a work of art as all the members are synchronized to the same rhythm to accomplish the task at hand. This can also be illustrated within the church as the individual members of Christ work together to accomplish the furtherance of the gospel.

Team unity is also about true selflessness. This spirit is so foreign in our sports world today, and yet for true team unity to be present, team members must demonstrate a true humility. How many times have you witnessed a very talented team of individuals that did not understand this basic concept? Rather than trying to make their teammate look better, it is all about them. Christ presents himself as the perfect picture of humility when He, who was God, became man. He gave up all his rights, privileges, and power for us.

He was obedient unto death, even the death of the cross. That was the ultimate sacrifice. He put Himself last, so we could be first. What are you willing to give up for your team? Are you really willing to put yourself last to help them be first? Do you really desire true team unity?

— VICKIE GROOMS DENNY, PH.D.

What is the cost of true unity? _____

_____

_____

18

FIELDS OF FRIENDLY STRIFE

" As iron sharpens iron, so one man sharpens another."

PROVERBS 27:17

At West Point, there is a famous quote by General MacArthur: "On the fields of friendly strife are sown the seeds that on other days and other fields will bear the fruits of victory." The belief that good athletes make sharp soldiers is the reason why all cadets are required to participate in a competitive team sport. The same principles for success on the athletic field apply to the battlefield. Left alone, a professional athlete or soldier will never amass a winning record.

As soldiers of Christ, we compete on a spiritual gridiron every day. If we are going to win consistently, we need teammates to encourage us when we fumble, to help us up when get tackled, and to celebrate with us when we score. Our enemy opposes us with minefields and ambushes along our path, seeking to prey on our weaknesses and shortcomings. That is why we also need a coach to challenge us to work on our weaknesses.

The Christian life is a team event. To be victorious requires the structure and resources found in a team of fellow believers, also known as a church. The pastor's exhortations on Sunday may make you uncomfortable, but this is the hallmark of every good coach. A good player will accept the coach's challenges with humility as long as they line up with the playbook for life; also known as God's Word. If it has been a while since you checked in with your team, perhaps you might consider showing up for practice this Sunday.

— AARON POLSGROVE

What teams do you need to be connected to in your life? _____

_____

_____

_____

_____

_____

_____

_____

_____

_____

_____

_____

_____

THE FIRE OF THE LORD

*" So Peter was kept in prison,
but the church was earnestly
praying to God for him"
ACTS 12:5*

My team played in the state semifinals my senior year of high school. The game was tied after regulation and then went to a shootout. As each person stepped up to take their shot, the entire team, coaches, and fans were cheering on that one player. Everyone was united behind him as he took his shot.

In Acts, Peter was in prison, and while he was there, brothers and sisters in Christ were praying for him.

Are we praying for others to succeed? When is the last time you prayed for a fellow believer going through a trial? Are we as excited when someone shares the Gospel as when our team wins a game?

It is important to be supportive of our teammates on the field, but it is much more important to be supportive of the teammates we have in life. We need to be supportive of our fellow brothers in sisters as we share the good news of the Gospel.

— NATHAN WADE

Do you pray for your teammates on and off the field? _____

_____

_____

_____

_____

_____

_____

_____

_____

_____

_____

_____

_____

_____

_____

RESOLUTION OF THE HEART

" Good sense makes one slow to anger, and it is his glory to overlook an offense."

PROVERBS 19:11 (ESV)

As an athlete, you typically come across acronyms, slogans, and phrases that are made to help and motivate – some of which have already appeared in the pages of this devotional. For instance there is: No Pain No Gain, KISS - Keep It Simple Stupid, Practice makes Perfect, etc.

As a child I remember playing youth basketball and a coach shared the 3 S's of shooting; Square your hips, Set your feet, Snap your wrist. Not too long ago, a former coach of mine, who is now a dear friend, shared with me the 4G's of Christ-like conflict resolution. In a time where stresses are running high and the pressures of life continue to grow, I am continually seeing more and more conflicts arise around me (not necessarily involving me).

Today, if you find yourself with a conflict or know a friend who may need some advice, use the 4G's to give you opportunities to glorify God, serve others, and grow to be like Christ. 1) Glorify God: trust and obey the words and feelings He lays on your heart to be at one with your brothers in Christ; 2) Get the log out: go to the heart of the issue and look where you may be at fault; 3) Gently restore: keep the issue between the parties involved and speak from your heart (Matthew 18:15); 4) Grow in Christ: be slow to anger (Proverbs 19:11).

Conflict is always around us and fills our world. If you are confronted today, try to remember the 4G's so you can glorify God, serve others and grow in Christ today.

— RYAN J. DINUNZIO

Blessed are the Peacemakers; does your ability to resolve conflict reflect your character in Christ?

_____

_____

_____

_____

_____

_____

_____

_____

_____

_____

THE ENABLING AND ENJOYMENT OF TEAM UNITY

" And over all these virtues put on love, which binds them all together in perfect unity."

COLOSSIANS 2:14

How can true team unity be obtained? We can only achieve true team unity with the help of the Holy Spirit. Since there is consolation in Christ and since there is comfort of love and because there is fellowship of the spirit, we can have true team unity. Because God first loved us, so we can love others. Because God shows us mercy, we can have mercy on others. Because of what God did for us, we can do for others. It is only because of the work of Christ and through his strength, that we can do this, but it is obtainable. In fact, the more one gets to know Christ and the power of His resurrection, the easier it is to have true team unity.

This type of response for team unity brings great joy. Paul says "fulfill my joy". Remember all the pain and suffering Paul was going through and in the midst of it all, he says knowing fellow believers are truly unified makes him happy. Have you ever been on a team that was really unified? Doesn't it bring out great joy and satisfaction knowing that everyone is there for one another?

Unity is summarized in three words: Love, Humility and Sacrifice. Team unity will not just happen. Everyone must be willing to love, demonstrate true humility and be willing to sacrifice. Do you really want an unified team? What are some practical examples of team unity that would encourage your teammates and coach? What would be really hard for you to do, but with God's help you could do? What will it take from you to have true team unity this season?

— VICKIE GROOMS DENNY, PH.D

What is the importance of unity in the Church? _____

_____

_____

_____

_____

_____

_____

_____

_____

A TRUE TEAM

" For in Him we live, and move,
and have our being;"
ACTS 17:28

Rick Hoyt was born with cerebral palsy. Being a quadriplegic prevents him from directly participating in sports. When he was 12, his family discovered that he enjoyed competitive sports when he chose "Go, Bruins" as his first typed words.

How can a person who loves competitive sports but is physically unable to participate in competitive sports compete in competitive sports? The only way possible is with the help of his father. During foot races, Dick Hoyt pushes Rick in a specialized wheelchair. In swimming, Dick swims while keeping a solid grip on the rope attached to the boat that Rick is lying in. In cycling, Rick rides up front in a specialized bike his father pedals. Rick once typed, "Dad, when I'm running, it feels like I'm not handicapped." The 2009 Boston Marathon marked the 1,000th event for Team Hoyt. That's the whole idea, though, they are a true team.

Like the Hoyts, we are also on a team if we have Christ. Because we've been born into sin, though, it is impossible for us, alone, to live the life God intended for us. The only reason we can now is because our Father enables us. He's part of our team. Without Him we can do nothing; through Him we can do all things.

— BURNEY SHEALEY

Have you ever looked at God as a teammate? _____

_____

_____

_____

_____

_____

_____

_____

_____

_____

_____

_____

_____

_____

_____

"Life without a purpose is a languid, drifting thing; every day we ought to review our purpose, saying to ourselves, 'This day let me make a sound beginning, for what we have hitherto done is naught!'"

— Thomas Lempis

"But the plans of the Lord stand firm forever, the purposes of his heart through all generations."

— Psalm 33:1

goal setting

PURPOSE, DIRECTION, RESPONSIBILITY

Before every season individuals (and teams) must go through a **goal setting** process. Having a goal creates a target at which to aim. Without a goal or destination, no matter how hard you try you probably won't go anywhere. Without a destination, how do you know when you have arrived? You don't. PURPOSE lets you build a plan. DIRECTION leads you to your goal. And recognizing your RESPONSIBILITY enables you to perform.

THE BULLDOG OF BERGEN

"The purposes of a man's heart are deep waters, but a man of understanding draws them out."
PROVERBS 20:5 (ESV)

If you haven't seen the movie, Cinderella Man, which chronicled a short portion of the story about James J. Braddock, nicknamed the "Bulldog of Bergen," or if you don't know his story, here's brief snipet: In the late 1920's, Braddock had a meteoric rise to the top of the boxing world, but quickly collapsed after some injuries. The stock market crash hit during that time, and like everyone else, Braddock hit hard times. He worked the docks on the North Jersey shore trying to make ends meet and take care of his family. He was broke and receiving government aid; then he got a second chance.

This time around he had a greater, more direct purpose; he fought from necessity to survive and provide. With this new purpose, Braddock beat the "unbeatable" Max Bear and became one of the greatest boxers of all time.

The Bulldog of Bergen struggled through hard times, but found purpose and prospered. His purpose was simple – fight to meet the need. Today, most of us are much more fortunate, but how often are we able to meet the need of someone else and then choose not to? Today meet the need. Whatever it is, meet it.

— RYAN J. DINUNZIO

What are you fighting for? What needs can you meet? _____

_____

_____

_____

_____

_____

_____

_____

_____

_____

_____

_____

_____

_____

_____

THE DUTY OF THE CHRISTIAN ATHLETE

" Jesus answered," I am the way, the truth and the life. No one comes to the Father except through me."
JOHN 14:6-7

The duty of a Christian athlete is no different than that of any other believer. We are commanded by God to share His message of salvation with the lost. It has been said that approximately 2 percent of American Christians regularly share their faith with others. Come on America, get off the bench and get in the game! If you are doing nothing or next to nothing, it is important for you to understand; we all will someday stand before Jesus and He will show us the many opportunities He gave us to help others. Jesus said; "I will tell you the truth, whatever you did not do for one of the least of these, you did not do for me." Matthew 25:45

Few of us will have Tim Tebow's athletic ability, but this should never stop us from sharing the good news of Jesus! We are all sinners, yet today we can stand before God and thank Him for giving His Son so that through His sacrifice we can spend eternity in paradise. Isn't this a story that deserves to be shared? I remember going 5-for-5 in a city championship fast pitch softball game many years ago. Unfortunately, we lost that game in extra innings when I could not catch a ball at the fence for the final out. Thankfully, Jesus is looking at our hearts and our love for others and not the scorebook. Take action, share His love story today!

— PAUL KELLY

Do you have an account of your responsibilities? Is the Gospel on there? _____

_____

_____

_____

_____

_____

_____

_____

_____

_____

_____

WHAT TIME IS IT?

*" Making the most of your time
because the days are evil."*

EPHESIANS 5:16

The above phrase became very popular because of Michael Jordan and the Chicago Bulls when they were winning so many NBA titles. Many teams in the early 1990s made that their rally cry, and it was seen before tip-off at most high school and college gyms. Athletes play games and they must always be cognizant of the time in the game. Why? Very simply — time does run out and the game will be over! Many games are won and lost because teams, players, and coaches misuse the clock. Vince Lombardi has the all-time quote on this matter, "We didn't lose the game, we just ran out of time."

We as believers are in a game, and God is keeping time (Ps.139:16), and the game of life will come to an end. But it's a good ending if you're a believer, because we win! In the meantime, God wants us to be in the game and make the most of the days He has given us.

What time is it?

1. It is time to turn on your light. Ephesians 5:8
2. It is time to walk the walk and talk the talk. Ephesians 5:1,4
3. It is time to live holy. Ephesians 5:3
4. It is time get in the game. Ephesians 5:15-16

God has even given us the tool to play — it's the Holy Spirit as we see in Ephesians 5:18,

"...be filled with the Spirit."

When the Holy Spirit controls us, we will never run out of time.

— JOHN ZELLER

Does your time have a direction? _____

_____

_____

_____

_____

_____

_____

_____

_____

_____

_____

_____

_____

WORKING FOR MEN OR GOD?

"each one's work will become manifest, for the Day will disclose it, because it will be revealed by fire, and the fire will test what sort of work each one has done."

I CORINTHIANS 3:12-13

On July 13, 1919, one of the strangest things happened in baseball. During a game, Chicago White Sox pitcher Carl Mays walked off the mound and quit. His reason? He didn't feel like he was getting enough support from his team.

I'm sure you've been there. You're working hard, trying to get things done and others who have promised to help are doing very little or nothing at all. I hear that sentiment echoed from ministers and lay people in the church a lot. But it happens in other areas of life as well.

It can be discouraging and can lead someone to stop what they're doing and, well, you know, just quit like Mays did 91 years ago on this very date.

Both actions (not helping much or at all, and quitting) are wrong, though. Why? Because our work or quality of work shouldn't be based on others' actions. It should be based on whether or not God has led us to do it. The energy, enthusiasm, motivation, etc., should come from knowing we are obeying God and doing what He wants so that we please Him, not in serving man and trying to please him.

— BRETT HONEYCUTT

Is it difficult to work for God and not yourself? _____

_____

_____

_____

_____

_____

_____

_____

_____

_____

_____

_____

_____

_____

_____

FROM FATHER TO SON

" But to all who received him, who believed in his name, he gave the right to become children of God, who were born, not of blood, nor of the will of the flesh nor of the will of man, but of God."

JOHN 1:12-13 (ESV)

For me it is simple, I have two true loves: Christ and the woman who I married. But when it comes to sports, I have one for each category: Sport? Soccer; NFL team? Dallas Cowboys; Hockey team? Buffalo Sabres; Athlete? Tiger Woods.

My true loves were gifts from God, but my love of sports and each intricate piece are what my father showed me to love. I fell in love with soccer, America's team, the Sabres, and some other sports-related things simply because I wanted to be so much like my father and wanted to share in his loves. Within sports, soccer is my father's and my first love. It will always be our greatest and deepest connection. Because of my desire to share my father's love, I was able to experience so much and create my own love for soccer.

What is our Heavenly Father's love? His children. Jesus tells us the greatest commandment is to love one another. How incredible would it be to share in our Heavenly Father's love? What would it do for our relationship with Him and for each other? Seek to love what the Father loves, His children. See what experiences unfold and the kind of love you develop on your own for your brothers and sisters in Christ.

— RYAN J. DINUNZIO

What are the responsibilities of love? _____

_____

_____

_____

_____

_____

_____

_____

_____

_____

_____

WHO DAT?

*" Being confident of this very thing, that He
who has begun a good work in you will
complete it until the day of Jesus Christ;"*

PHILIPPIANS 1:6 (NKJV)

Trivia question: Which NFL team played its first game on Sept. 17, 1967? Hint: There's something super about this team. If you guessed the New Orleans Saints, who won the 2010 Super Bowl, you're right. On Sept. 17, 1967, the New Orleans Saints played their first NFL game and lost 27-13 to the Los Angeles Rams.

And more than 40 years later, the Saints, who endured 20 consecutive seasons without a winning season (1967-1986) and had only eight winnings seasons before last season, finally made it to their first Super Bowl — and won. It took a while, but they finally made it to the top.

It's sort of like our life as Christians. Not everything starts out well, and it may take a while to get where we need to go and experience what God has for us, but if we follow God's plan the end result can be amazing — or super.

Are you struggling with God's plan for your life? If so, ask God to give you the strength to continue on the path He has for you, or ask Him to guide your steps and then give yourself completely to following Him. You won't regret it.

— BRETT HONEYCUTT

Do you feel God is giving you direction? If so, are you headed that way? _____

_____

_____

_____

_____

_____

_____

_____

_____

_____

_____

_____

_____

_____

POSSIBLE LIVING

"So we make it our goal to please him..."
II CORINTHIANS 5:9

The biblical translation of goal is "aim." On the converse, sin means to miss the mark. Have you ever shot a bow and arrow?

Well, I wanted to be Robin Hood as a kid. I wanted to shoot someone else's arrow out of the air or slit my opponent's arrow down the center. Adidas' slogan has been 'Impossible is Nothing'. You know it is a good one when Kevin Garnett (one front face for Adidas) responds to the question "How do you feel after winning this years NBA title?" He replies by yelling "Impossible is Nothing!"

What's really at the center of the goal for him? Was it the ring? Was it feeling like he is now a complete player heading to be a certified Hall of Famer?

What is at the center of what you aim for in this life this side of heaven? What do we take aim at in whatever we do?

Luke 1:37 said it best of Mary, a virgin, and Elizabeth, the old, barren cousin of Mary when they had children six months apart: "Nothing is impossible with God." Jesus being born helps us begin to grasp what 2 Corinthians 5:14-15 says: "...it is Christ's love that compels us...that those who live should not live for themselves, but for Him who died for them and was raised again."

Is our faith's center aim to please the One who did the impossible? Let Jesus be Lord of everything and watch Him do the impossible.

—JEAN-RENE TASSY

"Aim small...miss small." Where is your aim? Are you close to the target? _____

_____

_____

_____

_____

_____

_____

_____

_____

_____

_____

_____

_____

LESSONS FROM THE COURSE

" I press toward the mark for the prize of the high calling of God in Christ Jesus."

PHILIPPIANS 3:14 (KJV)

I was at a meeting in Texas several years ago and played in a golf tournament. I really enjoy the game, but I'm not very good. So for me to play well, I need to warm up before I begin.

The night before, there was a drawing for a driver and I won. So I was excited to hit my new club, but I didn't have the chance to warm up. That day, I was in the last group to tee off. There was another group, not connected to our meeting, waiting behind us and standing on the championship tees. The group I was with seemed to have a contest for the shortest drive. I approached my ball, took a big swing and missed the ball. Wow! I backed up, took another swing and I hit the ball a whole two inches. Wow, again!

I backed up, started over and now everyone was waiting and watching anxiously. I took another big swing, and it felt great. But then the ball hit a tree about 20 yards away and bounced right back in front of my feet. Now, I really had a lot of people waiting on me to get off the tee. So I teed it up one more time, determined to hit that crazy, little, white ball. Well, this time, I hit it about 80 yards straight up in the air and it came almost straight down about 20 yards in front of the tee box. Finally, I got in my golf cart as people laughed and gave me a hard time. It was all in fun, though. I drove about 60 feet, stopped my cart and started all over again trying to connect with that ball.

I know you are probably feeling bad for me, and that's fine, but all I needed was to warm up. In your spiritual life, have you ever thought about what you are driving for, and where you are headed? Just like me on the golf course, I made several mistakes but I kept swinging. I did not let all the noise and banter stop me from staying on course. It was a little rocky and very humbling, but the reminder here is to drive for and find true success in Jesus. Don't quit when it seems tough or hard in life, just keep swinging.

— ROBERT WALKER

What are some distractions from your direction? _____

_____

_____

_____

_____

_____

_____

_____

_____

HEAVENLY TREASURES

" Whoever loves money never has money enough; whoever loves wealth is never satisfied with his income. This too is meaningless."

ECCLESIASTES 5:10

When the nation was frenetically trying to discover Lebron James' next career move in early June 2010, former NBA player Darryl Dawkins made an interesting comment.

"He should go where he thinks he'll be happy," said Dawkins in a story by the Associated Press. "Make the right decision for your family and get as much money as you can..."

Get as much money as you can?

Society has always placed wealth on a pedestal. As Christians, however, we should live differently. Our focus should be outward (Where can I have the most impact for God's kingdom?) instead of inward (Where will I make the most money?) Even if it means taking a pay cut or not being as "happy" by the world's standards, what matters most is our effectiveness for God's kingdom.

King Solomon, the author of Ecclesiastes, was the definition of wealth in the ancient world. At the end of his life, however, he realized how meaningless it was. In Ecclesiastes 2:17 he says, "All of it is meaningless, a chasing after the wind. I hated all the things I had toiled for under the sun, because I must leave them to the one who comes after me."

We must leave everything we have on earth. Heavenly treasures, however, last for eternity.

— STEPHEN COPELAND

Do your earthly responsibilities distract you from your Christian responsibilities?

_____

_____

_____

_____

_____

_____

_____

_____

_____

_____

FULFILLING PURPOSE

*" Listen to advice and accept instruction,
that you may gain wisdom in the
future. Many are the plans in the
mind of a man, but it is the purpose
of the Lord that will stand. What is
desired in a man is steadfast love..."*

PROVERBS 19:20-22 (ESV)

John Wooden once said, "For an athlete to function properly, he must be intent. There has to be a definite purpose and goal if you are to progress. If you are not intent about what you are doing, you aren't able to resist the temptation to do something else that might be more fun at the moment." What he said is something I have always believed.

Playing sports, like life, is pointless without purpose. In football, you play to dominate for space and score more points. In soccer, you play for more goals. As an athlete, you train to increase your ability and play at higher levels; without these purposes sports would be meaningless.

In the same fashion, life is meaningless without purpose. For so many people, they amble through life with no faith, no identity in Christ, and no purpose. For us as Christians, we have a simple purpose – we were created for the glory of God, and everything we do is to glorify Him.

Look deep at what you are doing, then find your intent and purpose and align it with the purpose God has given you. With this you can stay the course, be focused, and reach high levels of excellence. Take coach Wooden's words and make them your purpose. He fulfilled his purpose on and off the court. Will you?

— RYAN J. DINUNZIO

What are your intentions? _____

_____

_____

_____

_____

_____

_____

_____

_____

_____

_____

_____

"Success always comes when preparation meets opportunity"

— Henry Harmtan

"Therefore, prepare your minds for action; be self-controlled; set your hope fully on the grace to be given you when Jesus Christ is revealed."

— I Peter 1:13

The PREPARATION is always longer than the performance, but the performance is what most often is noticed. You must be READY as an athlete when the opportunity to perform arises. In the same light, we should always be ready and preparing the way for Christ's return. To be successful in the season, you must put in time and effort in the **preseason.**

PREPARATION

" ...but in your hearts honor Christ the Lord as holy, always being prepared to make a defense to anyone who asks you for the reason for the hope that is in you; yet do it with gentleness and respect,..."

I PETER 3:15

Joe Paterno once said, "Failing to prepare is preparing to fail."

All throughout sport, it is common knowledge that those who prepare best usually have the most success. Preparation can take many forms in sport; film study, strategy, physical training, a good night's rest, an ice bath, an abundant training table, listening to music, etc.

However it is, athletes are constantly asked to be prepared – prepared for training, games, situations in games and so on. It becomes so routine for athletes, it becomes second nature.

How well and how often do we feel truly prepared? The question I ask is in regards to our heart. How often have you been asked why you are different or why are you filled with joy?

When you are asked these questions, are you prepared with more than just simply saying, "Christ!" It's a great answer, but are you prepared for the variety of roads that answer can lead you down? Can you defend your faith? Are you prepared for the daily spiritual battles with the devil? Is time with Christ, time in the word, time with God and time in prayer second nature to you? Preparation is key for any battle – whether physical or spiritual.

— RYAN J. DINUNZIO

What does your preparation look like? _____

_____

_____

_____

_____

_____

_____

_____

_____

_____

_____

BE READY

"David said to Saul, 'Let no one lose heart on account of this Philistine; your servant will go and fight him.'"
I SAMUEL 17:32

Will you be ready if you are called into the game at a moment's notice? Athletics are a lot of fun and I enjoy just about every sport. I have played competitively in soccer, baseball, basketball, wrestling, track and football. I have also enjoyed playing all types of recreational sports like tennis, horseshoes, golf, bowling, fishing, hunting and many others.

However, if you are going to be good at any of the above, it takes practice. If you are playing on any type of team you have to be ready all the time. A player injury can change the course of your season or even your life, but only if you are ready.

When I think of being ready, I think of Kurt Warner, a former NFL MVP and Super Bowl champion. In 1999, Warner was the backup quarterback for the St. Louis Rams. Before that he spent time in NFL Europe, and worked at a supermarket after being cut from professional teams.

That 1999 season, however, St. Louis' starting quarterback, Trent Green, went down with an injury and head coach Dick Vermeil chose Warner to replace him. Since that time, Warner broke and set many NFL records. He went from stocking shelves to winning a Super Bowl. How did it happen? He always prepared to play and stayed ready.

Are you ready? When Jesus puts you on the front line, will you be prepared and ready to battle? If not, prepare by praying and reading God's Word daily. Be ready in season and out of season.

— ROBERT WALKER

Do you have a readiness for your opportunity and the return of Christ? _____

_____

_____

_____

_____

_____

_____

_____

_____

_____

_____

OVERCOMING IS NO ACCIDENT

" Who shall separate us from the love of Christ? Shall trouble or hardship or persecution or famine or nakedness or danger or sword? As it is written: ' For your sake we face death all day long; we are considered as sheep to be slaughtered.' No, in all these things we are more than conquerors through him who loved us."

ROMANS 8:35-37

When Mine That Bird won the 2009 Kentucky Derby, it was the second biggest upset in horse racing's most prestigious event. At the rear of the field early in the race, the jockey made a tremendous move to squeeze through a small opening. After a huge burst of speed to pass the leaders, the race was won. Mine That Bird may have been a long-shot, but the win was no accident — talent, preparation, and a great application of strategy proved to be the winning formula.

You may feel like the odds are stacked against you in your Christian walk. You may feel like God is distant or that your attempts to serve Him are empty. Life's circumstances may feel overwhelming. So how do you overcome?

We overcome in much the same way Mine That Bird did. Time spent in God's Word provides the foundation and knowledge needed "so that the man of God may be thoroughly equipped for every good work." (I Timothy 3:16-17). Seeking God in prayer and asking for the direction of the Holy Spirit provide much needed direction. Correctly applying your talents, abilities and spiritual gifts results in works of service for God that are completely satisfying because they are focused on God's purposes rather than our own.

How is your spiritual training? Overcoming spiritual adversity is a matter of good preparation, responding to the Holy Spirit, and applying God's strategy. Luck has nothing to do with it.

— PHILLIP BLOSSER, PH.D.

Are you training for adversity? _____

_____

_____

_____

_____

_____

_____

FEEL IT

" My soul yearns, even faints, for the courts of the Lord; my heart and my flesh cry out for the living God."

PSALM 84:2 (ESV)

One of my favorite things in all of sports is the National Anthem. This may sound odd, but when I hear it, I really only can associate it with the start of games. From a young age, watching my uncles play professional soccer, the anthem marked a spark of emotions and the anticipation of what was to come—the exhilaration of the stadium noise, the fans, the goals, and the sheer pleasure of the spectacle of sports.

As I matured and reached collegiate and professional levels, it was my turn to stand at midfield and listen to our nation's anthem; it still sparked emotion. It was and always will be a trigger. The feeling that rushed through me was still that of anticipation, but it was different. Now it was anticipation of the task at hand, the feelings that would drive me for 90 minutes; I developed a routine that still is with me; my body instinctively moves to certain bars of the song in a certain manner. It was my preparation; it was my few final minutes to let the truths I know of soccer ready me to play while it drove my emotions to a point of almost euphoric pleasure.

Though my playing days are done, the routine is the same; anytime I hear the national anthem; those feelings of anticipation come back. Yet, that anticipation for the start of a game is nothing compared to my anticipation for the return of Christ. Let yourself be filled today with the emotions of anticipation; see what happens. Feel the coming of Christ; feel the power of redemption; feel His love, and feel His grace.

— RYAN J. DINUNZIO

What sort of anticipation do you have for Chirst? _____

_____

_____

_____

_____

_____

_____

_____

_____

_____

DEFLATED

*" All these are empowered by one
and the same Spirit, who
apportions to each one
individually as he wills."*
I CORINTHIANS 12:11 (ESV)

For the most part, spots are played with balls. The majority of these balls are made of leather and have rubber bladders filled with air; there are soccer balls, footballs, basketballs, volleyballs, rugby balls, etc. It is common, when purchasing these balls in the store, for them to be flat or deflated. Everyone knows that balls without air are essentially useless. Have you ever tried to dribble a flat basketball, throw a deflated football or juggle an empty soccer ball?

Much in the same way we can look at ourselves, and apply this theory. We cannot carry out our purpose for God if we are not filled with the Holy Spirit. It is essential that we are filled with the Holy Spirit so that we are completely useful in furthering God's kingdom. But as you know, no ball stays filled once you begin to use it. Every so often, as time passes, it loses some air and needs to be refilled. We, too, work in the same way, and need some refilling now and again.

Each and every day make sure you are pumped up and ready for the field of play.

— RYAN J. DINUNZIO

What needs to be done for you to be ready to play? _____

FILM STUDY

" ...humble yourselves under the mighty hand of God, that He may exalt you at the proper time, casting all your anxiety on Him... Be of sober spirit, be on the alert. Your adversary, the devil, prowls around like a roaring lion, seeking someone to devour. But resist him, standing firm in your faith..."

I PETER 5:6-9

Peyton Manning is regarded as one of the sharpest football minds in the game. Many experts feel he has so much success because of his ability to read opposing defenses; it is often said that no quarterback has managed audibles and the line the way he does.

How does he do it? Film study. Manning spends 10-15 hours a week studying opposing defenses. He studies the habits of the defensive coordinator and his play calling; he studies the tip-offs; he studies the formations, and he even studies individual defenders and their tendencies, strengths, and weakness. Manning becomes an expert on opposing defense's schemes and tactics; he knows his enemy.

As followers of Christ, we must know and prepare ourselves for Satan so that "you may be able to stand against the schemes of the devil" (Eph. 6:11b). It is our responsibility to study to be like Manning and to be alert enough to pick up the blitzes of the devil. Are you studied enough to call an audible when necessary? Can you see the devil's cover package? Call out your hot route to Christ today.

The mismatch where you know your guy is open...

— RYAN J. DINUNZIO

Are you able to confidently call "audibles"? Is your confidence in Christ? _____

_____

_____

_____

_____

_____

_____

_____

_____

STRENGTH IN GOD

"The Mighty One, God, the Lord, speaks and summons the earth from the rising of the sun to the place where it sets. From Zion, perfect in beauty, God shines forth. Our God comes and will not be silent . . ."

PSALM 50:1-2 (ESV)

Of everything I ever had a coach say to me, this is by far the one I have kept closest to my heart as a player, and again as a coach: "Don't worry when I am talking or yelling to you. You should be more concerned when neither of those two is happening."

It may seem harsh, but the bottom line is this: if a coach is talking to you or yelling at you, they are doing so because they care and want more from you, even if what they are saying is negative. When they are not doing either, it's because they don't care any more or don't expect any more.

I think God works in a similar way. His love is not conditional. So when He is yelling at you (figuratively speaking), He must be trying to get your attention even if He is rebuking or "punishing" you. He has a purpose. I don't think we should ever be fearful or hurt, or feel unloved by God. He is speaking to us no matter the fashion, yelling in anger or whispering in love. I know for certain I would rather have God yelling at me than not saying anything at all.

As you walk through your day, if you hear God, listen and be confident, even if He is "ripping in" to you. He does it because He loves and wants more for you. So listen.

— RYAN J. DiNUNZIO

Are you in the middle of a preseason chew out? What is He saying? _____

_____

_____

_____

_____

_____

_____

_____

_____

_____

_____

_____

ALWAYS BE PREPARED

" But know this, that if the goodman of the house had known in what watch the thief would come, he would have watched, and would not have suffered his house to be broken up. Therefore be ye also ready: for in such an hour as ye think not the Son of man cometh. Who then is a faithful and wise servant, whom his lord hath made ruler over his household, to give them meat in due season?"

MATTHEW 24:43-45 (KJV)

My daughter Hannah is a figure skater. She enjoys it and has excelled at it. Before she began, I knew nothing about the sport, so I had a steep learning curve. One thing I did notice was that you are all alone on the ice; no one can help you or do it for you.

I have played and coached mostly team sports. Unlike other sports, in figure skating there are no weekly games or matches. You see skaters practice all year long, many going before school and sometimes after school, as well. You will spend one year practicing for three or four, two-minute productions. Think about that. You practice daily, for one entire year, for thousands of hours, for a total of maybe four shows and eight minutes total. That is a lot of dedication for such a short program.

Unlike figure skating, we have daily opportunities to showcase our faith talents. Yes, we need to practice and grow in our faith, but we don't have to wait for a few chances to share our faith or be an encouragement to others. We are given opportunities each day, so let's take advantage of that by looking for and asking God to prepare us for them.

— ROBERT WALKER

What does it mean, or look like, to always be ready? _____

GPOD

" And he withdrew from them about a stone's throw, and knelt down and prayed...there appeared an angel from heaven, strengthening him."

LUKE 29:41-43

Early on in our athletic careers, we are guided to psych ourselves up for the big game. It is a tough concept to teach and figure out, because for most of us it is very different. Looking back on the various teams I have been on, and the hundreds of teammates I've had, I can think of dozens upon dozens of different ways guys got pumped up. The most common, though, was through music, but even that was different for each person. It ranged from classical, jazz, heavy metal, gangster rap, Gospel, contemporary Christian, etc. and seemingly every genre, every volume, every artist, all over the spectrum. Listening to music is the most common practice while getting ready for a game. It's played in arenas and stadiums, and now with the beauty of the iPod each player can customize what they listen to as they warm up or sit in the locker room.

Pregame pump-up is critical. Even Christ employed it before some of His most challenging moments. You read in the Bible that He was off alone praying, speaking to His Father. Essentially His earphones were plugged into the G-Pod. No matter the situation, being plugged into the G-Pod always had Christ prepared for victory.

As you prepare for the various "big games" in your daily life, are your earphones plugged into the G-Pod? The thing you need to know is that it is always the newest version, with the most space, the most music, and the best quality sound. Plug your earphones in and listen.

— RYAN J. DINUNZIO

*What helps your preparation for worship?*_____

_____

_____

_____

_____

_____

_____

_____

_____

_____

PREPARATION THROUGH PATIENCE

" But David said to Saul," Your servant has been keeping his father's sheep. When a lion or a bear came and carried off a sheep from the flock, I went after it, struck it and rescued the sheep from its mouth. When it turned on me, I seized it by its hair, struck it and killed it. Your servant has killed both the lion and the bear; this uncircumcised Philistine will be like one of them, because he has defied the armies of the living God. The Lord who delivered me from the paw of the lion and the paw of the bear will deliver me from the hand of this Philistine." "

I SAMUEL 17:34-37

Lets go back to the beginning of the Brett Farve saga, when he had just retired from the Green Bay Packers. Can you imagine how frustrating the situation was for Aaron Rodgers? Favre retires and Rodgers is named the starter. Great. But then Favre wants to play again and he hems and haws leaving Aaron in a state of flux. One minute Aaron was confident he would start, the next minute, he could have been a backup again. Well, we all know Aaron received his chance to shine. But this story is similar to that of David.

How frustrating would this be? - Jesse, David's father, was instructed to bring ALL his sons so one could be chosen as King, David was left behind. When David eventually got his chance, he was anointed king. However, despite being anointed with oil as the King, he was sent back to the fields to shepherd his flock. Not exactly what one would expect after being anointed King.

Years later, while the Israelites were fighting the Philistines, a 9 ft. giant mocked and cursed God and God's army. David was used by God to slay the giant. The time David spent in the fields protecting his sheep developed his character and faith in God. This character and faith in God are what empowered David to take on and kill Goliath.

Like David, the hallmark of your faith will not be found in one great act. Rather, you (like David) must willingly wait and walk the rocky roads of daily preparation. Through this, God will develop your character to match your calling.

— BRIAN PAYNE

How does patience affect your preparation? _____

_____

_____

" Life's most urgent question is: What are you doing for others?"

— Martin Luther King, Jr.

" ...and my spirit rejoices in God my Savior, for he has been mindful of the humble state of his servant. From now on all generations will call me blessed, for the Mighty One has done great things for me – holy is his name.

— Luke 1:47-49

regular season

We are called to SERVE daily, SACRIFICE ourselves for others, and do all of this with HUMILITY. Pride can easily cause an athlete to fall, and inhibit a follower of Christ from growing. Thinking of others more than ourselves is extremely difficult. This is the **regular season** for Christians, because we are to serve, sacrifice, and be humble always.

FREEDOM TO SERVE

"Then I heard the voice of the Lord saying, 'Whom shall I send? And who will go for us?' And I said, 'Here am I. Send me!'"

ISAIAH 6:8

In the above passage in Isaiah we see such a willingness to do something for God. We also see that in I Samuel 3 where it says, "The Lord came and stood there, calling as at the other times, 'Samuel! Samuel!' Then Samuel said, 'Speak, for your servant is listening.'"

That tenderness and giving up of one's will is always so refreshing to see, even when reading this for the 100th time. For me, it's refreshing because there is a freedom that comes from surrendering to Christ's will – a freedom we can only know when we do this.

This same freedom can be seen in the story on Chad Pennington, the former quarterback of the Miami Dolphins.

Listen to what he says about football: "Football is still an important part of my life, but it's a facet of my life where I need to be used by the Lord, not (for me) to use football. It's so easy in our business and our sport to get involved with the negative and get involved in all the different human intricacies of the game to where it just can drag you down and beat you up. There's such a freedom and sense of peace when you don't look at it that way. You can just wake up each morning and say, 'Ok, Lord, use me. Whatever that is, I'm Yours, just use me.'"

Let's begin today, and each day, by saying, "Ok, Lord, use me. Whatever that is, I'm Yours, just use me." Then we will begin to experience the freedom God offers us.

— BRETT HONEYCUTT

How does God want to use you? _____

_____

_____

_____

_____

_____

_____

_____

_____

_____

_____

WE NEED TO BE COACHABLE

" All Scripture is inspired by God and profitable for teaching, for reproof, for correction, for training in righteousness; so that the man of God may be adequate, equipped for every good work"
II TIMOTHY 3:16-17 (NAS)

To have all the talent in the world is meaningless if one does not work at improving. To be able to be great at anything, one must first admit that he does not have all the answers. Athletes learn from experience. But the successful ones also learn from coaching and their willingness to be coached. They are willing to hear constructive criticism on where they may be able to improve their game. They are not too prideful to be shown how to get better at something. Their desire to be the best allows them to be willing to listen to what they may not want to hear.

As Christians, we must take a similar approach. We don't have all the answers, but fortunately we know who does—God. The great thing is that He has given us His Word which is a blueprint for how we are to live and how we are to approach things. "All Scripture is inspired by God and profitable for teaching, for reproof, for correction, for training in righteousness; so that the man of God may be adequate, equipped for every good work" (2 Timothy 3:16-17). If our hearts are open, the Word can teach us, correct us, but most importantly train us up in righteousness. As verse 17 makes clear, we as men and women of God can be adequately equipped for every good work. But if we let pride get in the way and turn to ourselves, we are doomed to failure. Just as the talented athlete who is unwilling to be coached, the Christian who is unwilling to yield and learn from the Word of God is doomed to failure. For a Christian to serve God effectively, we must surrender all areas of our lives to Him. God is an expert in all things, and He knows more than us in every area of our lives.

— BRENDAN HANDEL

Are you allowing God to coach you? How? _____

_____

_____

_____

_____

_____

_____

DYING DAILY

" I affirm, brethren, by the boasting in you which I have in Christ Jesus our Lord, I die daily."

I CORINTHIANS 15:31 (NASB)

Wiley Petersen, one of the best bull riders in the world, is a Christian. He understands that his mission in life is to glorify God in whatever he does so that God's Kingdom can be advanced.

To do that, though, he also understands he has to die to the flesh daily as Paul says in I Corinthians 15:31. Basically, we have to daily submit ourselves to God and ask for His help to "walk in the Spirit" so that we do "not fulfill the lust of the flesh" as Galatians 5:16 says. Alone, we're no match against Satan and the world.

Petersen, who we feature in Sports Spectrum on pages 18-19, had this to say about living for Christ: "It's an everyday thing. Everyone has to get up each morning and say, 'I'm living for Jesus today. Yesterday is gone. Tomorrow is here.' Crucify the flesh and walk in the spirit. That's the challenge. Wherever you are in life, God's got you there for a reason. And He wants you to share His love with them...just stay focused on being obedient to Him and cling to Him."

Those are the keys: Die to the flesh daily, walk in the spirit daily, share Christ's love daily, stay focused daily and cling hard to God daily. You get the picture. It's a daily thing to live for Christ.

— BRETT HONEYCUTT

What prevents you from a daily death? _____

_____

_____

_____

_____

_____

_____

_____

_____

_____

_____

_____

_____

_____

IN THE RING

" But I say to you who hear: Love your enemies, do good to those who hate you, bless those who curse you, and pray for those who spitefully use you."

LUKE 6:27

During my lifetime, I have received racially prejudiced physical and verbal assaults. This led to feelings of insecurity, even to the point of contemplating suicide. As a perceived remedy to my problems, I turned to the martial arts for self-defense.

Over the years, I fought many opponents, and what was common in every altercation was that each of them was really a battle in an invisible ring...the spiritual realm. Ephesians 6:12, states, "For we do not wrestle against flesh and blood, but against principalities, against powers, against the rulers of the darkness of this age, against spiritual hosts of wickedness in the heavenly places."

It is imperative that we create for ourselves a daily regimen of wholeheartedly submitting to God's will over our own in order to become more Christlike; eliminating religious and racially segregated barriers.

By putting God's Word into practice, learning to swallow our pride, we become equipped to love our enemies...even in the ring.

The next time your ego is challenged, or your pride is hurt, how will you respond? Remember that your coach and trainer Jesus Christ is in your corner.

— B.T. WEST III

Sometimes a trainer needs to cut his fighter's eyes so he can see. What does Christ need to do for you to see past your pride?

_____

_____

_____

_____

_____

_____

_____

_____

_____

_____

_____

_____

THE VALUE OF SACRIFICE

" Greater love has no one than this, that
he lay down his life for his friends."
JOHN 15:13

When the Arizona Cardinals made it to Super Bowl XLIII, former team member Pat Tillman was remembered by the media and his fans since he likely would have been playing for the Cardinals if he was alive. His story is well known: a promising young safety who broke the franchise record for the most tackles in 2000. In May 2002, eight months after the 9/11 attacks and after completing the 15 remaining games of the 2001 season that followed the attacks (at a salary of $512,000 per year), Tillman turned down a contract offer of $3.6 million for three years from the Cardinals to enlist in the U.S. Army with his brother Kevin. After completing his training, Pat Tillman joined another team—the elite U.S. Army Rangers. In April 2004, he was tragically killed by friendly fire while on patrol with his unit in Afghanistan.

I heard a radio commentator say recently that Pat Tillman should be inducted into the Pro Football Hall of Fame. Flushed with emotion and patriotism his co-host "one-upped" him and said Pat Tillman belonged in the human being hall of fame if one existed. In a society that values money and material possessions, Pat Tillman's sacrifice certainly seems extraordinary; but Pat Tillman was not the first professional football player to die in combat. After being chosen Rookie of the Year in 1968, Bob Kalsu of the Buffalo Bills entered the Army and later died in action in 1970 in Vietnam.

While Pat did not profess Christ, his act represented the truth Jesus spoke about in Luke 12:15 when He said, "One's life does not consist in the abundance of the things he possesses." At one point in his NFL career, Tillman turned down a five-year, $9 million contract offer from the St. Louis Rams out of loyalty to the Cardinals. The media may feel they can assign a dollar amount to his sacrifice and worship him as a hero because of his promising career and the fact that he turned down a lucrative contract. But as believers, we know the only one deserving such praise is Jesus, who was killed as a ransom for many, then rose again so that whoever believes in Him will not perish, but have eternal life.

— AARON POLSGROVE

How can you live a sacrificial life for Christ? _____

_____

_____

_____

_____

_____

_____

SEEK HUMILITY

" For whoever exalts himself will be humbled, and whoever humbles himself will be exalted"

MATTHEW 23:12

My junior year at Wheaton College my roommate was a great basketball player. The 6-8 center had worked extremely hard both on the court and in the weight room (he went from190 pounds his freshman year to 230 pounds his junior year). The hard work paid off as well, as he earned all-conference and all-region honors his junior year. However, as remarkable as that was, it was something he said to me one day that impressed me even more. One day in our room he said to me, "Dave, don't let me get too cocky. It's easy to get caught up in basketball and get hot-headed. I don't want that."

In Matthew 23, Jesus scolds the Pharisees for their arrogance, and reminds us to stay humble. God desires for us not to become conceited, but to rely on Him. James 4:10 reminds us of this: "Humble yourselves before the Lord, and he will lift you up."

In whatever we do, we must remember that all our abilities are God-given. Our success pleases God, but will you let your accomplishments go to your head, or will you be like my roommate and seek humility?

— DAVID NOELL

What is humility to you? _____

_____
_____
_____
_____
_____
_____
_____
_____
_____
_____
_____
_____

LOVE OR PRIDE

" If I give all I possess to the poor and give over my body to hardship that I may boast, but do not have love, I gain nothing. Love is patient, love is kind. It does not envy, it does not boast, it is not proud."

I CORINTHIANS 13:3-4

Looking back on the teammates and captains on my teams throughout my playing career, I realized that the attitude of the team was usually the same as the attitude of the captains and best players. The teams that had good players who felt entitled, usually played with that kind of spirit. They expected every call to go their way, they complained when they had to do something they didn't like, and they usually were quick to yell at a teammate. One word that didn't characterize them was love. When I had captains who cared about each player and didn't put themselves on a platform, that attitude affected the whole team.

In 1 Corinthians, Paul points out that love and pride do not go together. I have never known anyone to be loving and proud. What would people say of us? Would they say you're loving? Do you put others first? Are you a servant leader? Or instead, are you proud? Do you always look out for yourself first? Are you the last person to volunteer to help with something? Do you consider players on your team not as good as you inferior teammates? What character trait do you have, love or pride? You can't have both.

— NATHAN WADE

How does your attitude affect the people around you? _____

_____

_____

_____

_____

_____

_____

_____

_____

_____

_____

_____

_____

SACRIFICE

"I beseech you therefore, brethren, by the mercies of God, that ye present your bodies a living sacrifice, holy, acceptable unto God, which is your reasonable service."

ROMANS 12:1 (KJV)

Many times in the game of baseball when a team is struggling to score or needs to advance a runner who is on base, the manger of the team will call on a player to lay down a sacrifice bunt, or a sacrifice fly. This is not what a player generally likes to do because it does nothing for his personal stats and appears on the scorecard as just an out he made. Yet the difference this player makes for his team, when he lays down a sacrifice bunt, is invaluable. By giving up his chance to get a hit for himself, the runner advances into scoring position, and sometimes comes across the plate as a result of the batter's sacrifice. It is then that the one who made the sacrifice is respected and admired for his willingness to give up his personal stats to help the team win.

Many times the manger of our lives, who is God, calls on us to sacrifice and to lay ourselves down for the cause of Christ's team. Our sacrifice may be a tremendous witness and testimony unto a lost world who needs to see something different in us, to see Christ in us. As Christ our great example laid down the highest sacrifice that could ever be given for our sins on the cross, let us learn from Him how to sacrifice ourselves when He calls on us to do so in whatever way it might be. In order to do that, though, we must first be a willing and obedient vessel that will lay ourselves down and forget about our own individual stats, successes or accomplishments to help the team win, Christ's team that is. What have you sacrificed for Christ's team?

— JASON BELCHER

What challenges your obedience of God? _____

_____

_____

_____

_____

_____

_____

_____

_____

_____

_____

A QUIET AND HUMBLE SPIRIT

*" For whosoever exalteth himself
shall be abased; and he that humbleth
himself shall be exalted."*

LUKE 14:11 (KJV)

PGA golfer K.J. Choi has been described as having a quiet and a humble spirit. Nothing more admirable could be said about anyone, especially a professional athlete who likely deals with all sorts of pride on an everyday basis.

In a way, Choi was exalted by the compliments of others (as Luke 14:11 says). Although he didn't receive a promotion or physical reward for his actions, he did receive the acknowledgement of having a humble spirit – which is far more important than position, power or monetary gain, especially if we believe the Bible.

In Colossians 3:12, we are told how much God thinks of humbleness when we are told, "Put on therefore, as the elect of God, holy and beloved, bowels of mercies, kindness, humbleness of mind, meekness, longsuffering;" and in James 4:10 we are told "Humble yourselves in the sight of the Lord, and he shall lift you up."

Having a humble spirit pleases God. So, if we struggle with pride, we need to first humble ourselves and bow down to God, and start honoring Him today with the quiet and humble spirit that He enjoys seeing in his children.

— BRETT HONEYCUTT

Is humility something you aim for? If so, how? _____

_____

_____

_____

_____

_____

_____

_____

_____

_____

_____

_____

_____

_____

A SERVANT'S HEART

" For even the Son of Man did not come to be served, but to serve, and to give his life as a ransom for many."

MARK 10:45 (KJV)

When I used to coach high school basketball, I found out quickly that the manager of the team was crucial. And over the years, I was fortunate to have some good ones.

Their to-do list seemed endless and they were always behind the scenes preparing so that the game was a success for the players and coaches. They would fill and hand out water bottles, hand out towels and ice packets, wipe the floor and prepare the gym, keep the stats for games and take care of uniforms. From a coach's perspective, they made everyone's life easier.

But as valuable as they were to the team, they were never the ones who people cheered and they were never interviewed by the newspaper. It takes a humble spirit and a servant's heart to be in that type of role.

So what is your role in your faith walk? Do you take the manager's role and serve others? If not, look for ways to help someone and let your example of encouragement and willingness to serve speak volumes to others. Remember that the manager may not get a lot of fanfare, but they play key roles by helping those who do.

What better example is there to follow than Christ?

— ROBERT WALKER

How do you shape a servant's heart? _____

_____

_____

_____

_____

_____

_____

_____

_____

_____

_____

_____

_____

_____

"Perseverance is not a long race; it is many short races one after another."

— Walter Elliot

"A patient man has great understanding, but a quick-tempered man displays folly. A heart at peace gives life to the body, but envy rots the bones."

— Proverbs 14:29-30

training room

Every athlete has experienced an injury in their career, which usually leads to spending time in the **training room,** or rehab center. If you've ever found yourself in that room as an athlete, you know you need PERSEVERANCE, and PATIENCE as you deal with your PAIN. As Christians we experience the same thing. We will find ourselves in Christ's training room seeking healing and recovery.

JUST SAY "THANK YOU"

*" For I am persuaded that neither death
nor life, nor angels nor principalities nor
powers, nor things present nor things
to come, nor height nor depth, nor
any other created thing, shall be able
to separate us from the love of God
which is in Christ Jesus our Lord."*

ROMANS 8:38-39

Disappointments are a common occurrence in all of our lives be they the result of a failed relationship, a missed promotion, news of a friends passing, or that an employee has deliberately disobeyed you. The fact is that heartbreak will be experienced by all of us at some point in our lives, but it is how we deal with adversity that builds our character.

Most of us remember the film, Apollo 13, where Ken Mattingly (played by Gary Sinise) was removed from flight status a mere 72 hours prior to the scheduled launch because of exposure to the German Measles. Little did Ken know at the time that his missing the launch would be so monumentally important to the safe return to Earth of Jim Lovell, Fred Haise, and Jack Swigert. Ken Mattingly may not have seen the global picture, but our Lord and Saviour certainly did.

In my own life I have failed at making the Canadian Olympic teams in 1992, 1996 and 2000, and I have also been passed over for promotions in the educational field. However, I have found great comfort in the knowledge and trust that I am a continual work in progress by my Heavenly Father. The Olympics came and went, and I was disappointed, but I realize that these things are temporal: He is eternal. In the darkest of nights, and on the loneliest of roads, I have found that He is ever-present and He is ever-caring. Every tear I have shed and every heartache I have experienced, He has been there to shoulder my burden. Our Father knows first-hand the pain experienced in seeing a Son die, but He also knows the bigger picture, and now, more than ever, I am persuaded.

— TERRY BURWELL

What is your response to personal pain and suffering? _____

_____

_____

_____

_____

_____

_____

THE WAITING GAME

" Wait for the Lord; be strong and take heart and wait for the Lord."

PSALM 27:14

When future Hall of Famer Roger Staubach was quarterbacking the Dallas Cowboys, he had a trusty backup named Danny White who doubled as the punter. White, who is a coach in the Arena Football League now, bided his time behind Staubach for four years before Staubach retired and White assumed the starting job. The hard thing for White and the Cowboys was the waiting. For White, it was waiting and not being able to play. For the Cowboys, it was waiting and not knowing whether or not White could step in and fill Staubach's shoes when Staubach retired. Could White handle the pressure? Would he be OK starting after not playing regularly for four years?

Can you imagine if White would have been impatient, demanded a release and was traded to another team? If he would have bolted, he would have missed leading the Cowboys to three NFC title game appearances, while being named All-Pro twice.

Imagine if the Cowboys had become impatient and forced Staubach out before he retired?

Staubach, who finished his career with four Super Bowl appearances and two titles, and he was selected to six Pro Bowls, racked up huge numbers during his final season. He set career highs for completions (267), passing yards (3,586), and touchdown passes (27).

Throughout the Bible, and especially the Psalms, we are told to wait on the Lord. God knows the best timing for us in everything. We think we know, but we don't. It could be God's way of saying, "I know best. Let me work and you'll see."

If you wait, you will see.

—BRETT HONEYCUTT

Do you leave margin in your life so you can be patient? _____

_____

_____

_____

_____

_____

_____

_____

_____

_____

PERSEVERE TO FINISH

"Suppose one of you wants to build a tower. Will he not first sit down and estimate the cost to see if he has enough money to complete it? For if he lays the foundation and is not able to finish it, everyone who sees it will ridicule him, saying, 'This fellow began to build and was not able to finish.'"

LUKE 14:28-30

It's the 1992 Olympic Games in Barcelona. British sprinter Derek Redmond is in the semifinals of the 400 meters. As he rounds the first turn, all of a sudden his hamstring tears and immediate pain sets in. Redmond, now limping, still heads for the finish line, but each step is tough. Then, aman runs out onto the track, despite efforts fromsecurity to stop him. The man is Redmond's father, Jim, who runs right to his son as Derek is limping to the finish line.

Jim Redmond reaches a helping hand to his child, and the pain becomes even more visible as Derek cries out in agony. However, both father and son refused to quit. With his arm around his dad, Derek reaches the finish line. Just because we decide to follow Jesus does not mean that our lives are going to be easy. Rather, as Hebrews 12:1 tells us, our lives are going to be more like a tough race requiring perseverance to complete. However, we do have Jesus there to help us when the times get tough, just as Derek Redmond had his father. Jesus will help us persevere through this tough life whether it's fighting through sin, or dealing with pain

With the help of his father, Derek Redmond finished the race. Will you finish the race? Will you persevere when the times get tough? Just remember, we have someone who will help us.

— DAVID NOELL

For you, is persevering a solo act? _____

_____

_____

_____

_____

_____

_____

_____

LIVESTRONG

*" More than that, we rejoice in
our sufferings, knowing that
suffering produces endurance, and
endurance produces character, and
character produces hope, and hope
does not put us to shame..."*

ROMANS 5:3-5

Whenever I read this verse I'm reminded of Lance Armstrong. I know it may seem outdated, but really it is a great example. If you don't know, Lance Armstrong is a cyclist who was diagnosed with cancer. After a two-year battle with the disease and after surgery, Armstrong returned to racing full-time and was far superior than the man he was before the diagnosis.

Seeing this challenge and still having a desire to race, Armstrong took his suffering and did not allow himself to be swallowed by it; he saw it as a chance to retool. He took that time off and began working to get back to where he was as a rider. But through the challenges and treatments it was hard to push through and get quality workouts. As he pushed through the pain and things began to get easier, he realized he had created a greater endurance than he had ever known. In achieving this, he developed a fortitude and character that would propel him to win an unprecedented seven consecutive Tour de France titles. Because of his accomplishment, he created a hope for so many cancer sufferers to believe anything was possible.

When you are faced with sufferings, do you rejoice? Does the way you handle your situation provide hope for others? The next time you feel down, turn back to Romans 5.

— RYAN J. DINUNZIO

Is there enjoyment in your suffering? _____

_____

_____

_____

_____

_____

_____

_____

_____

FOR SUCH A TIME AS THIS

" And who knows whether you have not come to the kingdom for such a time as this?"

ESTHER 4:14

In May of 2003, Jeff Torborg was fired as manager of the Florida Marlins. In that same year, the Marlins went on to win the World Series. But Torborg wasn't bitter then, and he certainly isn't bitter now.

While the Marlins were chasing the pennant, Jeff Torborg was at his summer home with his wife. One afternoon while painting, he heard a mysterious sound coming from the bay near their home. He came down from the ladder and started running down to the dock. Not seeing anything and still unsure of what he'd heard, he continued to the edge of the dock. Once there, he saw a toddler in the water about 15 feet away from the dock, and the waves were quickly pulling the boy out to sea. Jeff and a nearby gentleman jumped in and were able to pull the boy to safety. Miraculously, there was no water in the toddler's lungs and he had no brain damage. In Torborg's words, "It was an unbelievable experience."

Two days later, the rescued boy's mother brought him to Torborg's home to thank him for what he'd done. Torborg describes receiving a hug from the toddler, "That little boy hugged me and my knees buckled and the tears started to come. We just know we were in the presence of a miracle. Thirty seconds more, and that little guy is gone, swept under the bridge."

Jeff Torborg's son Gale, who was fired as a Marlins coach on the same day his father was fired summed it up, "Dad ...you were meant to be there for that little boy."

The next time you find yourself being uprooted, stay vigilant because God might simply be relocating you in order to accomplish something much bigger than you can imagine.

— TODD GREEN

Are there any areas in your life where you are running out of patience? _____

_____

_____

_____

_____

_____

_____

_____

_____

HOW WILL YOU FINISH?

"Therefore, since we have so great a cloud of witnesses surrounding us, let us also lay aside every encumbrance and the sin which so easily entangles us, and let us run withendurance the race that is set before us, fixing our eyes on Jesus, the author and perfecter of faith, who for the joy set before Him endured the cross, despising the shame, and has sat down at the right hand of the throne of God."

HEBREWS 12:1-2 (NASB)

Do you remember seeing or reading about Joe Namath leading the Jets to the improbable win against the Colts in Super Bowl III, or the four titles that Franco Harris helped the Steelers win in the 1970s? Or guys like Roger Staubach leading Dallas to two titles in the 1970s, and John Elway finally winning and leading Denver to two titles in the 1990s?

But did you know that Namath ended his career with the Los Angeles Rams and only played four games in 1977, or that Harris ended with the Seattle Seahawks and rushed for only 170 yards in eight games? They didn't finish their playing careers that well, although they eventually were elected into the Hall of Fame.

On the other hand, Staubach ended his career with the Cowboys after playing in his sixth Pro Bowl (he set career highs for completions, passing yards and TD passes that season), and a year after winning the Super Bowl. Elway ended his career after winning his second straight Super Bowl, earning MVP of the game and being elected to his ninth Pro Bowl. Both also were elected to the Hall.

How will you finish and be remembered? Will people only talk about the beginning of your life or will they talk about the beginning and ending? Will you finish poorly and skate into Heaven, or will you run all the way through the finish?

Please God by beginning and finishing strong.

— BRETT HONEYCUTT

Is the beginning or the end of your walk more important? _____

_____

_____

_____

_____

HE'S STILL WORKING ON YOU

" In fact, though by this time you ought to be teachers, you need someone to teach you the elementary truths of God's word all over again. You need milk, not solid food!"

HEBREWS 5:12

In 1955, a Brooklyn Dodger rookie pitcher made his major league debut, but it wasn't something to remember. He tied a MLB record by throwing three wild pitches in the first inning. He would also get spiked in a play at home and he didn't get a decision in the 4-3 victory against St. Louis. In three years with Brooklyn and the Kansas City A's (neither team had moved to California yet), he played in only 26 games, 20 of those as a reliever, and had a career record of 0-4, with one save and a 6.48 ERA. But if you knew that pitcher was Tommy Lasorda, you would also know it wasn't the end of the story.

Lasorda would go on to manage the Dodgers for 21 seasons, win two World Series, four National League pennants, be selected NL Manager of the Year twice, and be inducted into the Baseball Hall of Fame. He would also have his No. 2 jersey retired and win an Olympic gold medal in 2000, against heavily favored Cuba, to become the first manager to win the World Series and a gold medal. He was also inducted into the Canadian Baseball Hall of Fame after posting a 107-57 record in the 1950s for Montreal, then a minor league team, and leading the club to five International League titles.

Like our lives, what we are doing at this moment isn't the end of the story. So, be encouraged if you're in a seemingly bad situation or going through tough times, and know that, if you're reading this, your story is still being written.

— BRETT HONEYCUTT

What challenges your patience as God continues to write your story? _____

_____

_____

_____

_____

_____

_____

_____

_____

_____

_____

FAILURE ISN'T FINAL

*" My flesh and my heart faileth:
but God is the strength of my
heart, and my portion forever."*

PSALM 73:26 (KJV)

With just a few minutes left in a tie game between Virginia Tech and North Carolina in Blacksburg, Virginia Tech's running back, Ryan Williams, fumbled the ball while being tackled and the ball was quickly recovered by North Carolina. That fumble recovery led to a UNC field goal that broke the tie and gave the Tar Heels a three point win as time expired. After the game Williams was quoted as saying. "Nobody can lift me up right now," knowing that he had probably cost the team the game.

I thought about Peter when he denied the Lord three times, just as Jesus said he would. The Bible says that Peter went out and wept bitterly after the cock crew. Peter knew he had failed the Lord and that he had blown it. I'm sure he was so grieved at what he had done, that he felt like no one could lift him up either. Thankfully, though, God doesn't see our failures the same way man does, for the Lord gave Peter the great privilege to preach the sermon at Pentecost that would see 3,000 souls saved. Though Peter failed, God gave him another chance to redeem himself. Though man might have given up on Peter and could have told him that God would never use him again, I'm glad that God gives us His forgiveness and picks us up from our fall and encourages us to get back up and keep going with Him.

Aren't you glad that failure is not final with the Father?

— JASON BELCHER

Have you failed in the past? Is there anything that you haven't forgiven yourself for? _____

_____

_____

_____

_____

_____

_____

_____

_____

_____

_____

_____

IT'S NOT ABOUT UNDERSTANDING, IT'S ABOUT TRUST

"At this, Job got up and tore his robe and shaved his head. Then he fell to the ground in worship and said: Naked I came from my mother's womb, and naked I will depart. The Lord gave and the Lord has taken away; may the name of the Lord be praised."

JOB 1:20-21

If you're a baseball fan you likely haven't forgotten Dave Dravecky, the San Francisco Giants pitcher who battled cancer in his throwing arm from 1988 to 1991.

Nearly a year after pitching in the National League Championship Series for the San Francisco Giants in 1987, doctors found a tumor in Dravecky's throwing arm. He had surgery on October 7, 1988, to remove part of the deltoid muscle and freeze the humerus bone. In less than a year, he was back in the majors, and on August 10, 1989, he pitched his first game for San Francisco since the surgery. He pitched eight innings to beat Cincinnati 4-3. Everything seemed fine. The following game at Montreal, though, things turned for the worse. After looking solid early on and pitching into the sixth inning, his humerus bone snapped while throwing a pitch. The incident was replayed over and over on television, and fans agonized along with Dravecky each time they watched it.

Dravecky would never return to the majors. The Giants won the National League pennant that season, and two years later, in the summer of 1991, Dravecky had his left arm and shoulder amputated. He wrote two books about the ordeal, *Comeback* (1990), and *When You Can't Come Back* (1992), with the latter reading like a Job-type experience with friends doubting his faith, Dravecky questioning why, and various other things surrounding his ordeal. But Dravecky came through it, clinging to his faith and coming out a stronger believer. It wasn't because he was a strong person. He was weak. We all are. But he had faith and sought God.

How do we react in similar situations? Do we give up? Do we turn to other "things" for comfort or healing, or do we turn to God, trust Him and seek His face no matter how much we don't understand or no matter how much it hurts?

— BRETT HONEYCUTT

Does your pain distract you from seeking God? _____

_____

_____

_____

REHAB

"Therefore lift your drooping hands and strengthen your weak knees, and make straight paths for your feet, so that what is lame may not be put out of joint but rather be healed. Strive for peace with everyone, and for the holiness without which no one will see the Lord."

HEBREWS 12:12-14 (ESV)

At some level of sport I am sure you have experienced an injury or two. Everybody does. Some of those injuries are serious, an ACL tear for example, or simple, like a sprained wrist. With most of our minor injuries we throw some ice on it. If it still bothers us when we are set to go again, maybe we put some tape on it.

In college, I can remember walking into the training room and seeing my teammates getting their ankles taped every day (for practice and games). Still, they would roll their ankles or be icing down from pain after we played. I always thought to myself, "Why not fix the issue?" I started thinking of that again when a TV commercial stated that on game day, the average NFL player uses seven yards of tape. Seriously?

Continually taping an injury will never solve the problem, it is a temporary solution that may even lead to another injury. The only way to get past the tape is to take time and rehabilitate the injury. That means strength training, range of motion exercises, etc. Diligence to this is the only chance any athlete has to recover.

What are you putting tape on each day? Do you have any nagging "injuries" that you are just taping up and continuing to play with? What do you need to examine and rehabilitate? The good thing for us is that we have Christ as a physical therapist, and the Word of God as our routine. Spend time and rehabilitate today.

— RYAN J. DINUNZIO

Christ is the greatest trainer. Where do you need therapy? _____

_____

_____

_____

_____

_____

"Nothing great was ever achieved
without passion."

— Christian Friedrich Hebbel

"The laborer's appetite works for him;
his hunger drives him on."

— Proverbs 16:26

WORK ETHIC, PASSION, COMMITMENT

To continue develping as an athlete you have to spend countless hours on the **training ground,** or practice field, in, and out of season. Your WORK ETHIC is representative of your PASSION and your COMMITMENT. As followers of Christ we always need to be training. Your work ethic should be unmatched, your passion unparalleled and your commitment in the right place - Jesus.

THE FIRE OF THE LORD

" Do not put out the Spirit's fire."

I THESSALONIANS 5:19

Whether you are watching a baseball, basketball or football game, you can count on one of the announcers mentioning or commenting about the inner fire of one of the players. The announcer usually uses the analogy of fire to emphasize the tenacity or intensity of a player to describe the burning fire inside the athlete. We all can relate to the inner drive it takes to compete.

However, when the Bible mentions fire, the focus is not us but the power of God. Fire is referenced quite often in the Bible. One example of fire used in scripture is in Exodus when the Israelites were wandering in the wilderness. God directed the Israelites by cloud during the day and protected them with fire at night. Exodus 13:22 says, "Neither the pillar of cloud by day nor the pillar of fire left its place in front of the people."

Just like God's fire was always with the Israelites, that same power of the Lord is always available to us. We can access the fiery power of God at any time. We can access it on the baseball diamond, the football field and on the basketball court. We can access it when we are physically or emotionally drained and feel like we have nothing left. And, most of all, we can access it when we are facing temptation, which God's fiery power can give us strength to conquer.

Intellectually, we as Christians are aware of the power of God, but we fail to use it. Why? For me, the reason is that I try to accomplish things on my own. It's never good, because, in turn, I put out the Spirit's fire. Often, it takes me to a point of total emotional or physical exhaustion before I rely on God's fire and not my own inner strength. My prayer for you and myself is that I will pray for God's fire more often on a daily basis and not rely on my own futile strength.

— TIM SEARS

What, or whose fire burns inside of you? _____

_____

_____

_____

_____

_____

_____

_____

_____

_____

_____

GOING THE EXTRA MILE

" If someone forces you to go one mile, go with him two miles."

MATTHEW 5:41

In Matthew 5:41, Jesus laid out a new way of living for people who want to follow Him. Those who chose to do so, must be motivated by love. This was a very hard way to live since they were under oppression by Roman rule. Love helps you to move when you feel like stopping.

This same teaching ought to motivate the athlete in today's world. One of the best ways an athlete can give testimony of Christ is by going the extra mile. This motivation comes from a heart that wants to uplift Christ and not from a selfish perspective. Consider these basic principles:

1. Go the extra mile during practice - Arrive early; help set up and tear down equipment.
2. Go the extra mile during the game - Be intense and aggressive; control your emotions and words. Submit to authority.
3. Go the extra mile in the clubhouse - Remember who you are and whose you are.

Your deeds, motivated by love, get others' attention. So many people in the world today do not live a life motivated by love. Just as in Jesus' day, the best witness is a life that places others ahead of yourself. Show love to someone today.

— JOHN ZELLER

Which of the 3 areas do you already do? Is it motivated by love? _____

_____

_____

_____

_____

_____

_____

_____

_____

_____

_____

_____

_____

WHAT IT TAKES TO LIVE FOR CHRIST

" In the presence of God and of Christ Jesus, who will judge the living and the dead, and in view of his appearing and his kingdom, I give you this charge: Preach the Word; be prepared in season and out of season; correct, rebuke and encourage—with great patience and careful instruction."

II TIMOTHY 4:1-2

Anytime you try to accomplish something, you must always know what it takes to complete the task. Great teams, great athletes, and great victories have some components that can help us athletically as well as spiritually. Let's look at principles that can help us accomplish all that God wants us to while we live for Him!

1. Preparation (vs. 2)—We all have known that failure to plan is to plan to fail. Check out how all through scripture most leaders went through a time of preparation. Moses did in Exodus, Paul in Acts, and the disciples walked with Jesus for three years. Know how to handle God's Word—get prepared! Get all of Jesus that you can get!

2. Focus (vs. 1)—Keep the goal in front of you at all times. Many times games are won or lost by lack of focus during the game or at a critical time. Satan uses this tactic to get our eyes off Christ and cause us to lose direction.

3. Patience (vs. 2)—Loss of patience usually means loss of emotion. You can't perform at your best when you lose patience. Patience is a sign of good discipline; they go together. Seldom do great athletes accomplish their goals without these two traits.

Spiritually you are in a marathon, not a sprint, and you will need patience and discipline to finish strong for Christ.

Walk in such a way that through preparation, focus, and patience people will see Christ.

—JOHN ZELLER

It's not just commitment to a goal that counts; it's commitment to each phase and element of reaching that goal. What area needs more commitment?

_____

_____

_____

_____

_____

VITAL DISCONTENT

" Not that I have already attained, or am already perfected; but I press on, that I may lay hold of that for which Christ Jesus has also laid hold of me."

PHILIPPIANS 3:12

Early in the 1989 Big Ten men's basketball season, the University of Michigan was playing against the University of Wisconsin. Michigan's Rumeal Robinson was fouled late in the fourth quarter and stepped to the foul line to shoot two free throws. With his team trailing by only one point, Rumeal only needed to hit one for a tie, and both to win. He missed both shots, however, allowing Wisconsin to upset favored Michigan.

Needless to say, Rumeal Robinson felt the weight of costing his team the game. While deeply disappointed, he didn't let his sorrow stop at the emotional level. Rumeal realized that he needed to be better prepared, in case he found himself in that same situation again. For the rest of the season, Rumeal stayed after every practice and shot 100 extra foul shots.

As a result, Rumeal was ready when he was fouled with three seconds left in overtime in the national championship game. He confidently stepped up to the foul line to shoot two foul shots. Rumeal calmly swished both free throws consequently winning the national championship for his team.

Rumeal was placed in a situation that revealed an area of weakness in his game and his discontent with this weakness drove him to do something about it. Someone once said, "There is no growth, without discontent".

Has God revealed an area of weakness in your personal life? If so, are you discontent with this weakness? Begin today to place the necessary disciplines in your life in order to bring about the growth God desires.

— TODD GREEN

Are you willing to work and turn your weaknesses into strengths? _____

_____
_____
_____
_____
_____
_____
_____
_____

COMMITMENT

" ...my dear brothers, be steadfast,
immovable, always excelling in
the Lord's work, knowing that
your labor is not in vain."
I CORINTHIANS 15:58

The pursuit of athletic excellence and what you are willing to do in order to be successful reveal your level of dedication. Just forcing yourself out of a deep slumber from the comforts of a warm bed to start training says volumes about how passionate you are for the sport. The main thing that will decide whether or not you succeed at reaching your goals is if you are ready to stay absolutely committed.

We all have different views on sports and where its importance lies in each of our lives.

While many of us will not personally participate in the Super Bowl, win an Olympic medal or experience similar elite levels of athletic achievement, we all have the opportunity to accomplish great spiritual success when we give ourselves completely to God. No matter what may be going on in our lives, our relationship with God requires us to be steadfast and devoted to Him. By staying the course and walking in His ways, we discover there are certain blessings that are inherently proportional to just how committed we are to God.

Who and *what* are you most dedicated for today?

— BILLY BARNARD

Is every aspect of your life committed to God? _____

_____

_____

_____

_____

_____

_____

_____

_____

_____

_____

_____

_____

NIHIL SINE LABORE

"The works of his hands are faithful and just; all his precepts are trustworthy..."

PSALM 111:7 (ESV)

If you asked me what my favorite soccer team is, I might pause for a moment, but ultimately my answer would be Manchester United of the English Premiership. I think they are the first professional soccer team I ever watched on TV, and, undoubtedly, my childhood hero, Ryan Giggs, played, and still plays for them (I bleive he is the most underrated player of all time. He's in his late 30s and started his career at 17). As a kid, anything I could read or learn about United, I would; books, videos, everything I could get my hands on. I wanted to learn what it took to play for them; I wanted to understand their history and what has led to their long run of success.

Most of their recent success can be attributed to the enormous talent the team possesses, but several signs point to the team's manager, Sir Alex Ferguson. He runs a tight ship and believes in a firm line; but most importantly he values work ethic above all things. For his entire 36-year coaching career, he has had a placard in his office of an old saying of dock workers, "Nihil Sine Labore" or "Nothing Without Work." It's simple, without hard work nothing will be accomplished or achieved.

So simple, yet so profound. This is relevant to every avenue of life: school, sports, work, but most importantly, our Christian walk. We must constantly work to grow in our relationship with God and hone our tools for discipling and sharing the love of Christ with others. Without this work, we can't fulfill the great commission. Today, work for the Lord.

— RYAN J. DINUNZIO

Where do you find strength to work beyond yourself? _____

_____

_____

_____

_____

_____

_____

_____

_____

_____

_____

WARRIOR'S CODE

" But you, keep your head in all situations, endure hardship, do the work of an evangelist, discharge all the duties of your ministry...I have fought the good fight, I have finished the race, I have kept the faith. "

II TIMOTHY 4:5-7

If you've ever seen any of the Rocky movies, you know they are famous for two things: 1) Rocky doesn't know how to block a punch; and 2) the music. The songs are often very motivational, and if you're not careful you'll find yourself wanting to get up and exercise or something like that.

A few weeks ago I found myself watching one of the chapters of the Rocky saga. One of the songs really caught my attention – even though I had heard it many times before. A line in the song says, "In the warrior's code there's no surrender. Though his body says stop, his spirit cries 'NEVER!'"

Thinking about this one phrase, I asked myself if I am willing to be God's warrior and engage in spiritual battle. I also questioned whether or not I put on the whole armor of God and engage in battle as God's warrior. But the toughest question was, "Do I allow my flesh to control me or do I call upon the Spirit of God to give me the strength to fight the battle?"

I stand convicted by my own questions.

— CHRIS BOGGS

Do you stand committed to God? Are you convicted to fight? _____

_____

_____

_____

_____

_____

_____

_____

_____

_____

_____

_____

_____

ARE YOU WILLING?

" And every work that he undertook in the service of the house of God and in accordance with the law and the commandments, seeking his God, he did with all his heart, and prospered."

II CHRONICLES 31:21

I love Gatorade commercials. I always think it's kind of funny when they show the athletes at the end of workouts and they are beaded in sweat It's the least natural sweat I have ever seen. The thing I like is the image of the athlete buckled over with nothing left to give.

I can remember the games I felt the worst after, were some of the best I played. I remember a 120-minute affair against Chivas USA that I played with a cracked foot. After the game I was totally and utterly exhausted, I could hardly walk, and the next day, I really didn't want to get out of bed. However, I knew that night and the next day (even though we lost) that it may have been the best game I had ever played, and possibly the best game we played as a team. It was such a rewarding feeling, that memory knowing I gave everything. It easily outweighed the temporary exhaustion.

Through your daily walk, are you willing to give it all? Do you find yourself exhausted? Are you "dripping sweat" having worked tirelessly to share to love of Christ?

"The vision of a Champion is someone who is bent over, drenched in sweat, at the point of exhaustion when no one else is watching." ~ Anson Dorrance

— RYAN J. DiNUNZIO

What does it mean to work with all your heart? _____

_____

_____

_____

_____

_____

_____

_____

_____

_____

_____

HOW WILL YOU BE REMEMBERED?

" Now I commit you to God and to the word of his grace, which can build you up and give you an inheritance among all those who are sanctified"

ACTS 20:32

On this date in 1925 (85 years ago), New York Yankee great and Hall of Famer Lou Gehrig hit the first of 23 grand slams he would compile in his storied 17-year career. The 23 grand slams are still a record, with the closest person (Manny Ramirez) needing three to break the mark.

Thinking of that mark brings three things to mind: The first time we did something significant, at least in our eyes, the longevity of something done well and how people remember us.

Baseball fans know Gehrig as the "The Iron Horse" for playing in 2,130 consecutive games without a day off, despite fracturing multiple bones, and for his tearful retirement speech in 1939 as he stood in front of fans at Yankee Stadium to tell them he couldn't play any longer because of a neurological disease, amyotriphic lateral sclerosis (ALS), that would later be known to most people as Lou Gehrig's Disease.

How will you be remembered? Will people remember your kindness or bitterness, helping others or helping yourself, your gentleness or harshness, a meek spirit or condemning one?

Take charge, be filled with the Spirit and begin to show Christ's love to a world that desperately needs Him.

— BRETT HONEYCUTT

What are you committed to leaving for others? _____

_____

_____

_____

_____

_____

_____

_____

_____

_____

_____

_____

SEEK AND PURSUE WITH PASSION

The young lions suffer want and hunger;
but those who (B) seek the
Lord lack no good thing.
PSALM 34:9-11

One of the common characteristics that is used to describe some of the sports' greatest heroes, Michael Jordan, Muhammad Ali, Mickey Mantle, Bobby Orr, Tiger Woods, Walter Payton, is heart.

At some moment, or several moments for that matter, these men displayed a great deal of heart and passion to achieve success. You could see the fire and determination in each when you looked into his eyes. It was a drive and a fire that burned deep inside that compelled them to push through all obstacles to reach the mountain top.

One of the other great things that can be said of all these men is they did it within the rules, and aside from Ali and Woods, they carried their teams with them. For these men during their respective careers, it was titles, cups, and championships they sought with a burning passion. All reached what they wanted.

What sort of fire burns inside of you? Is it white hot and able to push you through every obstacle and distraction? Is it focused enough in the center of your heart to keep you from taking a short cut in life? I know that if it is anything like the fire that existed in the men mentioned above, you will find what you seek.

— RYAN J. DINUNZIO

What is it that you seek? _____

_____

_____

_____

_____

_____

_____

_____

_____

_____

_____

_____

"And when we think we lead, we are most led."

— Lord Byron

"Now, Lord God, let your promise to my father David be confirmed, for you have made me king over a people who are as numerous as the dust of the earth.' Give me wisdom and knowledge, that I may lead this people, for who is able to govern this great people of yours?'"

— II Chronicles 1:9-10

LEADERSHIP, GOD'S AUTHORITY

LEADERSHIP is a quality that is difficult to teach; it needs to be fostered, learned, and cultivated. The best way to gain understanding of leadership is to look at other leaders. But to really lead, you need to follow - you need to follow GOD'S AUTHORITY. He provides the strength, protection, power, patience, and other elements you need to be an effective leader. Only teams with great leadership make the **playoffs**.

LEADERSHIP SERVES

" Have this mind among yourselves, which is yours in Christ Jesus, who, though he was in the form of God, did not count equality with God a thing to be grasped, but made himself nothing, taking the form of a servant, being born in the likeness of men. And being found in human form, he humbled himself by becoming obedient to the point of death, even death on a cross."

PHILIPPIANS 2:5-8 (ESV)

I love watching the playoffs in any sport. For me, this seems to be the time where true leaders emerge. It is an incredible thing to see players rise to the standard of excellence needed to win championships; but most remarkable is seeing leaders rise to the occasion to lift their teams, but more importantly teammates.

It is key for leaders in sports to make their teammates better, but more importantly they need to be unselfish. We see that today with the likes of Lebron James and Kobe Bryant; Kobe has plenty of championships, but his leadership has always been questioned because of his selfish reputation. Lebron may be the best in the game, but he is unable (at this point) to serve his teammates and help elevate their games in order to get past teams that are simply playing better. With that said, I ask you, "How do you lead?"

It doesn't matter if you are a CEO, a team captain, a student, a stay-at-home mom, you can be a leader. It's not what you lead, it's how you lead. Christ served first. Through servanthood, He led. If we are to make disciples of all nations, we need to be leaders; to lead we must serve. I challenge you to assess where you lead and how you lead. See where you can serve those you lead better. True biblical leadership takes a heart of obedience and humility.

— RYAN J. DINUNZIO

Who are you serving? Are you leading them too? _____

_____

_____

_____

_____

_____

FEELING REJECTED

"The Lord said to Gideon, 'With the three hundred men that lapped I will save you and give the Midianites into your hands. Let all the other men go, each to his own place.'"

JUDGES 7:7

Rejection. The men referenced in that last sentence were excluded from the victory God planned for the Israelites. Gideon starts with 32,000 troops, already outnumbered by the Midianites. But Gideon sends 22,000 scared men home; then God tells Gideon, "You still have too many men."

So Gideon sends 9,700 battle-ready and willing fighters home. The text omits the details, but we can put ourselves in the shoes of those men cut from the army. "Gideon, you're already outnumbered, and you mean to tell me the army is better off without my support?" Ouch.

In sports, rejection and failure are not possibilities; they are certainties. On one of my favorite motivational posters, Michael Jordan recounts the failures in his Hall of Fame career. If MJ fails, what does that say about the rest of us? We are all capable of monumental failure; and there's no denying rejection is painful.

Feelings of failure and rejection come from unmet expectations we place on ourselves because of our perspective and not on the awareness of God's greater plan. Being cut from a team, removed from the starting lineup or suffering a season-ending injury can cause us to pause and allow the Holy Spirit to renew or change our priorities. Our perspective is day-to-day, and in the daily grind we can overlook a priority critical to God's plan. Fortunately for us, God's plan is long-term.

Reading the full account in Judges 7, God's plan wasn't about strength in numbers; God was allowing the Israelites to witness His magnificent authority. Rejection becomes an opportunity to reconnect with God by petitioning for wisdom in our circumstances.

— ALAN MORGAN

How do you change your perspective to see God's power? _____

_____

_____

_____

_____

_____

_____

TRUE POWER IN CHRIST

" By his power God raised the Lord from the dead, and he will raise us also."

I CORINTHIANS 6:14

Much of the golf swing is about power – rotating your body until you are fully torqued, the weight on your back foot, then whipping through the ball at impact. It's humorous how many people think that swinging hard is the origin of power within the golf swing. It's about torque. Without it—without power—golfers have to settle for bogeys on long holes.

Life is the same way. As we stand on the tee box gazing at a green in the distance, we are sometimes deceived to believe that we have to swing hard to reach the green. People find power in money, fame, sex, or the pursuit of the American dream. Like swinging hard, we are too easily deceived by power.

When you swing out of your shoes, you'll find trouble. You may plunk one into the water or hook one into the trees. It produces inconsistent results and leads you down a hazardous journey. Similarly, if you pursue alternative sources of power in life, you will always find yourself in a place you don't want to be.

Real power comes in Christ. The same power that raised our Savior from the dead now lives in us through the Holy Spirit. If you know the right way to swing a golf club, it's foolish to abandon what you know is true and try to swing hard instead. Through the Holy Spirit, there lies incredible power. But we too often ignore it. Live by the Spirit and stay on the straight and narrow.

— STEPHEN COPELAND

Is it possible to experience God's power without knowing the truth?

CHAMPIONSHIP PEDIGREE

" ...if you have faith as small as a mustard seed, you can say to this mountain,' Move from here to there` and it will move. Nothing will be impossible for you."

MATTHEW 17:20

Benchman Tyler Evans didn't need the starting lineup to have his name in eternal lights for his university. The senior may not have been the University of Findlay's planned go-to guy, but when it counted, he was clutch.

Evans sank a long-distance jumper to lead Findlay to its first NCAA Division II title and a perfect 36-0 season in April 2010. He finished the game with four points. His game-winning trey was the Oilers' biggest bucket in school history.

Evans was usually the second man off the bench, not your MVP-type. This reminds one of some low-key, yet legendary men of the Word. Although they are mentioned minimally, their impact can still be far and wide with depth.

How about Jabez? Three verses, but legendary now with God granting his request to have kingdom influence and impact expanded. How about Benaiah? Everyone knows him, right? Well a lion sure did. He killed a lion in a pit, one-on-one, and King David gave him great leadership roles in response. Stephen gets a few nods of reference in Acts as a follower of Christ, most notably as, "a man full of faith and of the Holy Spirit." Now that's an epitaph.

Tyler Evans may be the most memorable Oiler in the history of Findlay basketball—or their sport's program in general. In a similar light, your name doesn't have to be mentioned often like Jabez, Benaiah or Stephen to have kingdom championship pedigree.

— JEFF PINKLETON

How does your leadership influence the "championship pedigree" of others? _____

_____

_____

_____

_____

_____

_____

_____

_____

_____

QUALITIES OF A CAPTAIN

*" For an overseer, as God's steward,
must be above reproach. He must not
be arrogant or quick-tempered or a
drunkard or violent or greedy for gain,
but hospitable, a lover of good, self-
controlled, upright, holy, and disciplined."*

TITUS 1:7-8 (ESV)

As a youth soccer coach, one of the biggest challenges I had each season was selecting the captain(s) of my team. For a long time I struggled with which method was better: having the players vote, me choosing, or a hybrid of the two. As a player, I had experience with each, and they all had some pros and cons. But over time, I discerned that it wasn't so much the method of selection, but the qualifications of selection that were critical.

Whether I chose, the players voted, or both, it was necessary that I defined the qualities and attributes that are necessary for good/great leaders; I never thought the Bible would provide the benchmark for leadership qualities for sports, but it did. As I delved into 1 Timothy and Titus, it was clear that Paul laid out 20 characteristics that are essential for all leaders, no matter what the venue is.

No one quality is more important and they are all essential. Today, take some time, review 1 Timothy 3:1-5 and Titus 1:7-8 and assess each of these characteristics in your own life; review your strengths and weaknesses and see where you can improve. Godly leadership starts right here, today.

— RYAN J. DINUNZIO

How can you work on these characteristics? _____

_____

_____

_____

_____

_____

_____

_____

_____

_____

_____

HUNG BY THE TONGUE

"The tongue also is a fire, a world of evil among the parts of the body. It corrupts the whole person, sets the whole course of his life on fire, and is itself set on fire by hell."

JAMES 3:6

Athletes at all levels need and require instruction, encouragement, and yes, correction. This is true for the kid walking onto the field for the first time all the way up to the most-experienced professional. But it's how the instruction and correction is administered that makes the difference. Coaches and parents can destroy a budding talent with undue or mean-spirited criticism (by the way, there is no such thing as "constructive criticism;" criticism is criticism).

James 3 compares the tongue to a fire. Fire can be classified as a "friendly fire" or a "hostile fire." A friendly fire, by definition, is one within its intended boundaries and/or being used for its intended purpose. A hostile fire is one that escapes its confines and destroys.

Fire is necessary just as instruction and correction are necessary for athletes and Christians. But don't let the fire of correction escape its intended boundaries and destroy the target at which it's aimed. Churches should be warmed by the words that proceed out of our mouth, not burned by gossiping, backbiting, rumors, etc.

The tongue can provide encouragement where it is needed; a challenge to be more Christ-like when it is needed; and correction when it is needed. But it can also destroy. Control the tongue and warm the Church.

— CHRIS BOGGS

God's words are perfect in His leadership. How do you rate your words as a leader? _____

_____

_____

_____

_____

_____

_____

_____

_____

_____

_____

BEFORE THE GAME

*" In the beginning, God created the heavens
and the earth. "*

GENESIS 1:1

After the 2008 Summer Olympics in Beijing had ended, Iwas still in awe of the opening ceremonies. The intricacies, the detail, the timing, the imagination, the artistry, and the innovation were all almost too much. What I sat in awe of for nearly two hours was only the final product. To learn that 16,000 people were used and spent nearly 16 hours a day for eight months in preparation, not to mention the three years for creation and chorography of the product, is jaw-dropping.

Just think all of that beauty and emotion for two hours. Amazing.

My astonishment grew themore I learned of the process which led to the product. Yet it makes me think of all that time and energy for a mere two hours. It in no way compares to the earth and heavens that God made, and that only took Him seven days.

Is it easy to overlook God's unparalleled design because we see it daily? Have you ever really pondered the process of creation? Looking at and thinking about what came before the Olympic Games, are you more amazed now?

— RYAN J. DINUNZIO

What is your daily reminder of God's power? _____

_____

_____

_____

_____

_____

_____

_____

_____

_____

_____

_____

_____

_____

_____

_____

_____

_____

LEADER BY EXAMPLE

" No one will be able to stand up against you all the days of your life. As I was with Moses, so I will be with you; I will never leave you nor forsake you. Be strong and courageous, because you will lead these people to inherit the land I swore to their forefathers to give them. Be strong and very courageous. Be careful to obey all the law my servant Moses gave you; do not turn from it to the right or to the left, that you may be successful wherever you go. Do not let this Book of the Law depart from your mouth; meditate on it day and night, so that you may be careful to do everything written in it. Then you will be prosperous and successful."

JOSHUA 1:5-8

Los Angeles Galaxy star Chris Klein doesn't boast about being a leader. It's clearly seen by his teammates.

"There are times when he's not happy with his performance or his playing time," says teammate Gregg Berhalter. "But in the locker room, he's the same person. He's not grumpy. He's not down on himself. He's not down on his teammates. He continues to lead through example and always give everything on the training field."

Like Klein, Joshua didn't have to tell everyone he was worthy of being a leader after Moses' death. God saw it in him, first when he said they could take the promised land, and then by his continued actions of trusting God.

Are you someone who can lead, but instead your life doesn't measure up? Today, start honoring God by being a man or woman who, first, seeks after Him and His ways. Whether you are a leader by example or you are a vocal leader, God and others will begin to take notice who you serve.

— BRETT HONEYCUTT

Who in your life is a leader that sets a good example? _____

_____

_____

_____

TRUE LEADERSHIP

" Brothers, if someone is caught in a sin, you who are spiritual should restore him gently. But watch yourself, or you also may be tempted."

GALATIANS 6:1

There was a wonderful article in *Sports Spectrum* magazine on Steve Smith and Ken Lucas. The story of these two is a story on forgiveness and leadership. As a huge Carolina Panthers fan I was so excited about the start of another year. I really felt we had a chance to do something great. Then, the story of the training camp fight was reported; how Smith had punched a defenseless Lucas. My first thought was that this is going to ruin our season. Then Lucas spoke up and didn't tear down Smith. He forgave him! That act of leadership brought the Panthers together, and they went on to have a wonderful season.

As hard as that would be to do, we are commanded to do so. Sometimes we get sidetracked by personal feelings or we want to have a grudge, but we can't. We are to build our Christian brother or sister back up because we never know when we may be in the same situation.

Are you holding grudges or letting those around you hold grudges against you? Be a leader and work things out. You never know when you may be the one needing forgiveness. Always show grace because Jesus always shows us grace.

— STEVEN STINSON

*Is forgiveness or grace preventing you from true leadership?*_____

_____

_____

_____

_____

_____

_____

_____

_____

_____

_____

_____

IMPOSSIBLE IS NOTHING

"For nothing is impossible with God."
LUKE 1:37 (ESV)

Being a soccer guy, it goes without saying that I prefer adidas over Nike, hands down. As a company, adidas has such a storied history. Recently, they have seen a small resurgence, and with their acquisition of Reebok they now are the official brand of the NFL, the NHL, the MLS, and the NBA. But more notable than this is their marketing campaign, "Impossible is Nothing," which I am sure you've seen. For the past three years they have run commercials with highlights of Muhammad Ali, a cartoon of David Beckham, still shots of Dwight Howard, and others, all followed by the words "Impossible is nothing." This campaign is meant to illustrate the stories of these sports heroes from humble beginnings to great success. In other words, stories of redemption. On the website these athletes share their stories and the overcoming of struggles.

It seems to me that adidas ripped this campaign straight from the pages of God's Word. Think of all the stories where impossible really is nothing, and all things are possible in God and Christ; Noah and the ark, Jonah and the whale, Daniel in the lions' den, the birth, resurrection and life of Christ, and the conversion of Paul. The impossible becoming possible is everywhere in the Bible.

If adidas can use a short tag line to inspire athletes, young and old, shouldn't we as believers be more inclined to lead and inspire non-believers and new believers with proof that only through God, impossible is nothing? Find your story, I know it's there, where God proved that impossible is nothing, and share it with someone today to encourage or inspire them in their relationship with Christ.

— RYAN J. DiNUNZIO

What can you not accomplish on your own right now that you haven't taken to God? _____

_____

_____

_____

_____

_____

_____

_____

_____

_____

" Excellence can be obtained if you:
...care more than others think is wise;
...risk more than others think is safe;
...dream more than others think is
practical; ...expect more than others
think is possible."

— Anonymous

" He is the Rock, his works are
perfect, and all his ways are just.
A faithful God who does no wrong,
upright and just is he."

— Deuteronomy 32:4

championship

EXCELLENCE, PERFECTION

The sign of EXCELLENCE for athletes and teams is a **championship**. With the amount of work, time, energy, and effort it takes to accomplish supreme success in the sports world, we see the value of that level of excellence. The same can be said of Christians. Just as athletes pursue a championship, we seek excellence in Christ and His PERFECTION.

WHO WILL HELP ME HONOR HIM?

*" Whatever you do, work heartily, as
for the Lord and not for men."*

COLOSSIANS 3:23 (ESV)

That verse has been my life verse for the past 20 years or so. These few words encompass so much. This verse started becoming significant to me late in my career as a soccer player and then early in my coaching career. God really began to drive them deep into my soul and mind.

Three things jump out at me when thinking about this verse:

1. God expects us to work hard at everything, not just Bible reading and prayer. In every area of our lives we are supposed to give it our all - studying, working, relationships, sports and seeing and loving God.

2. Not only do we have to work at everything; we must do it with all our heart. God tells us to give maximum effort always, not 15 percent or even 99 percent, but 100 percent effort in all we do. I like to think of this as God's call for us to be excellent - all the time. We need to shine for Him.

3. The last thing this verse says to me is when you do everything well, all out, and with reckless abandon, that you need to do it for God and not for others or ourselves. Our desire in everything we do must be to exalt the name of Jesus and lift His name above everything.

God wants us to do everything to the best of our ability to honor Him!

— MARK STEFFENS

What does your best look like at... home... work... school... church, etc.? _____

_____

_____

_____

_____

_____

_____

_____

_____

_____

_____

_____

_____

_____

When Excellence is Missing the Mark

" *Be perfect, therefore, as your heavenly Father is perfect.*"
MATTHEW 5:48

Vince Lombardi. Winning. Excellence. Missing the mark.
Something is out of line there. The first three lines fit well together. The last not-so-much, but Lombardi will tell you it does.
Lombardi's first message to his sub-par Green Bay Packers after taking over raised the bar.
"Gentlemen, we are going to relentless chase perfection, knowing full well we will not catch it, because nothing is perfect."
He continued, "But when we miss the mark, we'll achieve excellence."
After many losing years in Packerland, Lombardi's ways led to the nickname, Titletown, for the Wisconsin city.
Neither you, nor I can achieve perfection. That's not an argument, but as we let the Holy Spirit do the work of grace and transformation in our lives, we can achieve the same type of excellence for our coach.
That's our way of reaching and climbing the benchmark of excellence.

—Jeff Pinkleton

How is your pursuit of perfection? _____

_____

_____

_____

_____

_____

_____

_____

_____

_____

_____

_____

_____

_____

_____

_____

_____

EXCELLENCE OR MEDIOCRITY?

*" Only let us live up to what
we have already attained."*

PHILIPPIANS 3:16

After Drew Brees led the New Orleans Saints to a Super Bowl title in 2009, it would be ridiculous to think he would happily settle for a .500 season this year. It just doesn't work that way. Once you reach the top, you no longer settle for mediocrity.

As Christians, we have already attained the ultimate reward in eternity. It's absurd to settle for anything less. In the above verse, Paul urges the Philippian church to "live up to what we have already attained." In other words, Paul wants them to live in the light of eternity — something they have already received on behalf of Christ.

But what does it mean to live in the light of eternity? Under Brees, the Saints were 7-9 in 2007, and 8-8 in 2008. After winning the Super Bowl a year later, it's fair to assume that Brees never wants the Saints to return to their mediocre past. Nor does he want his team to forget their Super Bowl victory. Why? Because they have attained excellence.

Similarly, Christians, when living in the light of eternity, should not slide back to their mediocre and complacent past. Nor should they forget about their first experience with Christ. Why? Because after someone encounters Christ, that person is destined for excellence — for he has attained eternity.

— STEPHEN COPELAND

Is excellence sustainable? _____

_____

_____

_____

_____

_____

_____

_____

_____

_____

_____

_____

_____

PATIENCE MAKES PERFECT

" But let patience have her perfect work, that ye may be perfect and entire, wanting nothing."
JAMES 1:4 (KJV)

I'm sure most of us have heard the phrase "practice makes perfect." But as you know, practicing something one time will not bring perfection. Even after a few practices, it is still likely that you will mess up on the very thing you've been practicing, but that doesn't mean that you're not on your way to perfection.

Any athlete would tell you that it takes practice after practice before perfecting any skill. It takes practice along with patience on the road to perfection. Continue practicing and give it time.

Our relationship with God can be like this sometimes. After giving Him our hearts, we expect perfection overnight in our lives and in our relationship with Him.

We "practice" by reading our Bibles, going to church, and doing those things that would help our relationship with Him to grow, but we make one mistake and it seems as though we've gotten nowhere! Now, what do we do? Well, first read 1 John 1:9, and then have patience! Keep reading and meditating on God's Word to let it get inside our hearts and take root. Once it has taken root, it will grow to produce results in our lives—results on the way to perfection.

— LEAH METCALF

*Is patience relevant to perfection?*_____

_____

_____

_____

_____

_____

_____

_____

_____

_____

_____

_____

MAKING THE MOST OF WHAT'S GIVEN

" From everyone who has been given much, much will be demanded; and from the one who has been entrusted with much, much more will be asked."

LUKE 12:48B

Watch Coach Danny Ford was just beginning to settle in after his second full season at Clemson. Following his debut in the 1978 Gator Bowl, Ford's Tigers had posted two mediocre records (and no national rankings) in 1979 and 1980. When Clemson took the field in 1981, no one outside the Palmetto State had high expectations for the upcoming season. In fact, the team wasn't ranked in the Associated Press Top 25 Poll. Yet, the Tigers had other plans, and just like their freshman defensive sensation William Perry, this team was destined for something really big.

Ford and the Tigers realized they had more talent than most people expected. Their mediocrity during the previous two seasons had allowed them to fly 'under the radar,' avoiding the preseason 'hype' that often distracts (and ultimately derails) so many good teams. Clemson walked through that season with an 11-0 record, beating nationally-ranked powerhouses Georgia and North Carolina along the way. Yet, when they were invited to play against perennial power Nebraska in the Orange Bowl on New Year's Day, most experts doubted Clemson's ability to cap the perfect season. In the end, Clemson secured the National Championship by winning 22-15. The win forever cemented Clemson's place in the college football world.

In life, we are often faced with situations where others may not feel as though we're capable of doing 'big' things. But with God's help, and by using those gifts and abilities He has graciously given, we can often prove our detractors wrong. Are you making the most of what God has given you, or are you settling for something less than your very best?

— COREY THOMPSON

What are the gifts God has given you? _____

_____

_____

_____

_____

_____

_____

_____

EVEN BETTER

I eagerly expect and hope that I will in no way be ashamed, but will have sufficient courage so that now as always Christ will be exalted in my body, whether by life or by death.

PHILIPPIANS 1:20

She waits at the start line with a sculpted physique. Her body and mind both poised to compete in a race that compels her to hurdle toward the finish line where she will either face victory or defeat. But regardless of the outcome, Yvana Hepburn knows her labor is not in vain. She has competed on the highest collegiate level in the 60-meter hurdles and 100-meter hurdles as an athlete at the University of South Florida. And yet she still presses on.

Even though her stop clock no longer ticks at South Florida, her race has not yet ended. Yvana also runs this race called life, hurdling obstacles, embracing victories, accepting defeat, all the while keeping her eye on a prize that can neither be won nor earned. It is a prize she simply receives, and she shares that prize through a legacy she has passed on to her teammates, both through her living testimony and through the Athletes in Action Bible study she led in the spring of 2010.

But Yvana's legacy is not one that remains in yesterday. As she now races toward Olympic-sized dreams, she envisions the legacy she will leave: the legacy of a lifetime.

As we run our own race, will we leave our legacy at the start line, or will we carry it with us to the finish?

— LEAHA SHAIKH

What legacy do you want to leave behind? _____

_____

_____

_____

_____

_____

_____

_____

_____

_____

_____

YOUR BEST FOR THE LORD

" For none of us lives to himself alone
and none of us dies to himself alone.
If we live, we live to the Lord; and if
we die, we die to the Lord. So, whether
we live or die, we belong to the Lord."
ROMANS 14:7-8

It was almost game time again, and like I had done so many times before throughout my high
school basketball career, I was praying. I asked God to help me do my best and realize that's all that I could do. When I was younger, I would get upset and even cry every time my team lost. I always took the blame for the loss. As I grew older, I was always very hard on myself, even if I knew that I had given my best effort. Eventually, I started to realize that my best effort was all that was required of me, so I asked God to help me realize this. God did help me, because I started to not be as hard on myself. I still gave my best effort and learned from my mistakes, but I realized that God only asks for our best. Romans 14:7-8 reminds us that we do indeed live for God, and not for ourselves. Therefore, when we work or strive to achieve a goal, we are doing it for God.

Let us live for God then! Do your best for the Lord in whatever walk of life you are part of. Don't be discouraged if you don't always achieve your desired results, but realize that your best for the Lord is all that is required.

— DAVID NOELL

Do you really believe your best is all that is required of you? _____

_____

_____

_____

_____

_____

_____

_____

_____

_____

_____

_____

_____

PERFECTION?

"For our sake has made him to be sin who knew no sin, so that in him we might become the riotousness of God."
II CORINTHIANS 5:21 (ESV)

As a perfectionist sometimes it is hard for me to settle for anything less. I had a P.E. teacher who once told me that the much spoken quote "practice makes perfect" is flawed. That in reality it should say, "Perfect practice makes perfect performance." As a follower of Christ I know I am not perfect and that Christ is the only perfect and pure thing ever to be a part of this earth. "Perfect games" in baseball and bowling come at the failures of others—batters' inability to hit the ball and pins' inability to stay standing. Christ's perfection came for the glory of His father and His willingness to build up others and be pure in what is right.

In our daily walk perfection is unattainable but it is worth striving for. The only way to even have a chance or coming close to perfection is to focus on practicing perfectly the love that is in Him.

— RYAN J. DINUNZIO

What does His perfect love look like? _____

_____

_____

_____

_____

_____

_____

_____

_____

_____

_____

_____

_____

_____

_____

_____

_____

_____

THE JOY SET BEFORE US

" If perfection could have been attained through the Levitical priesthood-and indeed the law given to the people established that priesthood-why was there still need for another priest to come, one in the order of Melchizedek, not in the order of Aaron?"

HEBREWS 7:11

The higher we set our goals, the harder we have to work to attain them. There is such a great feeling of accomplishment after winning a championship or reaching a goal. To have finally attained something you've worked so hard for brings immense joy.

As athletes, we run suicides (back and forth, up and down the court) until our legs begin to cramp, lift weights until we can't feel our muscles any longer, and daily train for hours in our sports. And why do we endure such pain? Because our focus is on the goal we want to attain—that joy set before us—the highest achievement of winning the championship or accomplishing our goal.

Our faith walk is similar. Do you long for the "highest" faith? Do you long for the faith to trust God in every circumstance, regardless of how it may seem? Do you long to rest assured, knowing that God loves you and that He has everything under control? Not only recognizing that He loves you, but also knowing that He has good things in store for you as well.

Let's fix our eyes on the "highest" goal Jesus—the Name above all names, the King of kings, the Lord of lords; and the Author and Perfecter of that faith we long for.

— LEAH METCALF

How do you aim for perfection? Is Jesus beside you?

MAKING COACH PROUD

"Continue in him, so that when he appears we may be confident and unashamed before him at his coming"
I JOHN 2:28

Sometimes at the school where I teach, students who have gone on to high school will come back to serve as "assistant coaches" for the sports teams they played on when they were in middle school. They always feel honored to come back and help out the head coach. When they've been there a few times, sometimes the coach will let the student lead warm-ups or part of a practice while he goes on to take care of other things. No pressure, right? Wrong. Of course there's some pressure there because the student wants to make sure the coach is pleased when he gets back. So he's going to work extra hard to make sure he does all he can to be secure in the job he's done while the coach was away.

Put yourself in the position of that assistant coach. You're working with the team for a period of time, and you have a job to accomplish. You want to make the head coach proud. God is our head coach. He has called us and placed us in a position to carry out a specific task before He returns. It's an honor for Him to have chosen us. We should do all we can to make sure we can be confident in and unashamed of the work we've done when He comes.

What work are you doing for the Coach? Will He proud of the job you've done so you can stand before Him confident and unashamed?

— KRYSTIL WADE

What is the excellence that you seek? _____

_____

_____

_____

_____

_____

_____

_____

_____

_____

_____

_____

"God loves each of us as if there were only one of us."

        – St. Augustine

"But the gift is not like the trespass. For if the many died by the trespass of the one man, how much more did God's grace and the gift that came by the grace of the one man, Jesus Christ, overflow to the many!"

        – Romans 5:15

awards banquet

GOD'S...GRACE, TRUTH, LOVE

Usually at the end of the season there is an **awards banquet.** This is a chance for teams, coaches and players to receive honor for what they have done or accomplished. What is greater, though, are the rewards we receive from God for doing nothing. We receive the honor of salvation and glory of everlasting life in God's Hall of Fame purely because of His GRACE, TRUTH, and LOVE.

UNCONDITIONAL LOVE

" If I speak in the tongues of men and of angels, but have not love, I am only a resounding gong or a clanging cymbal. If I have the gift of prophecy and can fathom all mysteries and all knowledge, and if I have a faith that can move mountains, but have not love, I am nothing. If I give all I possess to the poor and surrender..."

I CORINTHIANS 13:1-3

I competed in track and cross country in college. One thing that took me a while to appreciate, though, was the support I had. Not just from my coaches and teammates, but from my parents.

My mom and dad lived in Charlotte, N.C., and I went to school in Virginia. I remember them driving to meets in Tennessee, eastern North Carolina, Virginia, Pennsylvania and New Jersey. They just wanted to see me and they just wanted to see me do something I enjoyed.

My mom reminded me of the time they came to Philadelphia to watch me run one of my last college meets. My dad was so excited that he couldn't sleep, so they left home at some crazy time close to or just after midnight. Even now, thinking of his excitement, is comforting.

Unfortunately, I didn't appreciate their show of love like I should have when I was in college. I'm not sure why I didn't. I did grow to appreciate it, though, but unfortunately, I appreciated it after my dad passed away. I regret that. I regret that I didn't show him how much I appreciated him driving four, six, eight and 10 hours to watch me run. When I ran only one race, it was only to watch me run for less than two minutes. Wow. He loved me so much that he would drive hours and hours to watch me run for less than 120 seconds. I regret that I didn't tell him how much that meant to me (even more so now as I write this).

The encouragement for you who are reading is to love, love deeply and show your appreciation to those who love you, especially God and Christ.

— BRETT HONEYCUTT

What does it look like to appreciate the love of God? _____

_____

_____

_____

_____

_____

_____

THE TRUTH WILL SET YOU FREE

" And that is what some of you were. But you were washed, you were sanctified, you were justified in the name of the Lord Jesus Christ and by the Spirit of our God."

I CORINTHIANS 6:11

A former basketball star at the University of Wisconsin, Katie was set to play on our Athletes in Action fall exhibition team when she called me the day before training camp with news of an injury. Many doctors had looked at her knee and found nothing wrong, yet she experienced a lot of pain while playing. She came to training camp and played through the pain as best she could the first few days.

At a team Bible study that first week, she felt led to share some of the tough things in her past with her teammates. She was nervous, having never told a whole group before. Though she feared rejection, the team showered her with incredible love and compassion. We could practically see the chains of bondage falling off as Katie took another step toward living in the light of Christ's forgiveness and love!

The next day at practice, Katie played with zero pain. Her knee was healed! She played in every practice and game from that day forward. The emotional healing God performed on her heart led to a physical healing of her knee. God showed us His ability to completely heal and restore!

How have you experienced God's healing touch emotionally or physically? What have you learned about God as a result?

— STEPHANIE ZONARS

What does sharing grace with others tell them about you? _____

_____

_____

_____

_____

_____

_____

_____

_____

_____

_____

ROUND 2

" Then he began to curse and swear, saying, ' I do not know the Man!' Immediately a rooster crowed. And Peter remembered the word of Jesus who had said to him, ' Before the rooster crows, you will deny Me three times.' So he went out and wept bitterly."

MATTHEW 26:74-75 (NASB)

On Sept. 21, 1956, the New York Yankees did something uncharacteristic for a team that seemingly won everything and scored at will. The Yankees stranded a record 20 runners on base that day and lost 13-9 to their nemesis, the Boston Red Sox. In the same game, though, Hall of Famer Mickey Mantle hit a home run more than 500-feet, the perfect example of the strength of that team.

It reminds me of Peter, the person who cut off the ear of Malchus, the high priest's servant, because he didn't want Jesus to be taken away to be crucified, and the same person who denied Christ three times. He was bold and brave in one instance, then weak and scared in another — and in essence, it all dealt with whether or not to stand up for Christ.

We see two sides of Peter — weak and strong — just like we saw two sides of the Yankees, who had the ability to do better but just didn't.

The bad part is that we all do good and bad, whether we're Peter, who obviously loved Christ or he wouldn't have risked his life to save him, or King David, a man after God's own heart who committed heinous sins. The good part is that Christ, like he did with Peter in John 21:15-19, forgives us and gives us second chances. Have you messed up and thought God couldn't use you? Be comforted by the God of second chances and read John 21 today.

— BRETT HONEYCUTT

Is God's forgiveness permanent? _____

_____

_____

_____

_____

_____

_____

_____

KING FOREVER

"The Lord is king forever and ever! The godless nations will vanish from the land."

PSALM 10:16

"Hoosiers" is one of my favorite sports movies of all time. One of my favorite scenes is in the first game where Coach Norman Dale benches a player for not doing what he is told despite the fact that everyone else had fouled out and only four players were left on the floor. The crowed was extremely upset with him for only playing with four and even one of his most loyal supporters told him, "I have a hard time believing that you know what you're doing." In the movie, the team struggled at the beginning of the season, but they finally got a hold of what Coach Dale was teaching them and ended up winning the state title. Even though things didn't look good, Coach Dale knew what he was doing.

In Psalm 10, the writer gives a picture of a very bleak situation. The wicked and the proud are hunting down the poor and they are getting away with it! Why doesn't God punish them? How could God allow this to happen? What is he doing? Yet in verse 16, the writer boldly states "The Lord is king forever". Despite all the evidence pointing in the opposite direction, the writer still realizes that God is the King and he is in charge! He knows what he's doing!

Even when everything in your life seems to be falling a part and it really doesn't look like God is intervening, just remember, "The Lord is king forever and ever!" He has it under control.

— JEFF WEAVER

How does this truth affect you? _____

_____

_____

_____

_____

_____

_____

_____

_____

_____

_____

_____

_____

_____

_____

THE ULTIMATE BAILOUT

*" When you were dead in your sins and
in the uncircumcision of your sinful
nature, God made you alive with Christ.
He forgave us all our sins, having canceled
the written code, with its regulations, that
was against us and that stood opposed
to us; he took it away, nailing it to the
cross. And having disarmed the powers and
authorities, he made a public spectacle of
them, triumphing over them by the cross."*
COLOSSIANS 2:13-15

Other than the NFL playoffs, March Madness is the best time of year. One of the best games of the 2009 tournament was the Villanova vs. Pittsburgh game. Villanova seemed to have the game in the bag with just a few seconds left. All they had to do was inbound the ball, get fouled and hit the free throws to ice the game. Then, the inbounder, Reggie Redding, threw an errant pass the length of the court that was stolen by a Pitt player who dribbled the ball up the court, was fouled and hit two free throws to give Pitt the lead with five seconds left. I can't imagine how Redding felt. I am sure he felt hopeless. His mistake was going to be a costly one. Then, after an amazing inbounds play, guard Scottie Reynolds from Villanova dribbled the ball to the lane and hit a fade away with less than a second left. The relief on Redding's face was easily seen.

I was bailed out like that one time. I was hopeless. I was playing a game that I was going to lose, and it was my fault. I was a sinner, and I was bound for hell. Just like Redding was going to have to accept the consequences for a bad pass, I was going to have to accept the consequences of my sins. Luckily for me and for you, Christ bailed us out. He took our sins and nailed them to the cross so that we could be forgiven. Now, I can walk around with relief on my face.

Have you been bailed out? Romans 6:23 says that the wages of sin is death, and that is what we deserve. Good thing for us it doesn't end there. It goes on to say that the gift of God is eternal life. Christ died on the cross to bail us out of what we deserve, which is hell. If you have not accepted this bailout, let today be the day. It is the best and most important decision you will ever make.

— STEVEN STINSON

What has the love of God bailed you out from? _____

114

PURE FORGIVENESS

" Bear with each other and forgive whatever grievances you may have against one another. Forgive as the Lord forgave you."

COLOSSIANS 3:13

There is nothing that shakes this world up more than forgiveness. The sporting world experienced that on June 2 after first base umpire Jim Joyce botched a call that cost Detroit Tigers' pitcher Armando Galarraga a perfect game. The replays clearly showed that Joyce was wrong.

Galarraga's response was mind-blowing to many. After Joyce saw the replays and realized that he was in the wrong, he approached Galarraga to apologize. Galarraga welcomed him with a hug.

"He really feels bad," Galarraga said of Joyce in an article by MLB Fanhouse editor Andrew Johnson. "He probably feels more bad than me. Nobody is perfect. I give a lot of credit to that guy. [An apology] doesn't happen. He apologized. He feels really bad. Nobody is perfect. What am I gonna do? His eyes were watering and he didn't have to say much. His body language said a lot."

Jim Leyland, the Tigers' manager had a similar response. He argued with Joyce after the game, but later praised the prestigious (now infamous) umpire and defended him. "That's the nature of the business, that's just the way it is," Leyland said in the same article. "The players are human, the umpires are human, the managers are human, the writers are human. We all make mistakes. It's a crying shame. Jimmy's a real good umpire, has been for a long time. He probably got it wrong."

There is nothing more captivating than forgiveness. Truthfully, aren't we all Jim Joyce? After all, we have all botched it. We've botched it big time. But still, our welcoming, loving, understanding Father is always there to give us a hug when we approach Him with genuine repentance — just as Joyce did.

— STEPHEN COPELAND

Do you need to seek more of the forgiveness of God? _____

_____

_____

_____

_____

_____

_____

_____

_____

LOVE CHANGES LIVES

" By this all men will know that you are My disciples, if you have love for one another."
JOHN 13:35 (KJV)

The evidence showed that Ken Lucas was a believer.

In the aftermath of Lucas having his jaw broken by teammate Steve Smith during the Carolina Panthers' training camp this preseason, Lucas forgave Smith and talked about both players being in Bible study together.

Remember what Jesus said in John 15:12? "This is my commandment, That ye love one another, as I have loved you." He commanded us to love each other. Loving someone isn't based on feeling. It's based on obedience. A hard pill to swallow sometimes, I know. But our love to Christ is shown in obedience.

Lucas asked how he could go to Bible study with someone and not forgive him, intimating a believer should always forgive.

In Luke 17:3-5, Jesus reminds us how often we should forgive: "Take heed to yourselves: If thy brother trespass against thee, rebuke him; and if he repent, forgive him. And if he trespass against thee seven times in a day, and seven times in a day turn again to thee, saying, I repent; thou shalt forgive him."

And Ephesians 4:32 reminds us how we should be toward people and, most importantly, that God forgave us, "And be ye kind one to another, tender-hearted, forgiving one another, even as God for Christ's sake hath forgiven you."

And what if we don't want to forgive? It's your choice, but Jesus tells us (Matthew 6:14-15) what will happen if we choose to go that route: "For if ye forgive men their trespasses, your heavenly Father will also forgive you: But if ye forgive not men their trespasses, neither will your Father forgive your trespasses."

Choose love *and* choose forgiveness. It's the best, and only way.

— BRETT HONEYCUTT

How can you respond to others with the same love and grace God has shown you? _____

_____

_____

_____

_____

_____

_____

_____

_____

_____

STANDING STONES

"Great is the Lord and most worthy of praise; his greatness no one can fathom."
PSALM 145:3-7

In 2009, the old Yankee Stadium was closed and the new Yankee Stadium opened. Monument Park, located behind the outfield wall, was moved to the new stadium and has monuments dedicated to legendary Yankee players like Babe Ruth, Lou Gehrig and Mickey Mantle.

The Israelites used to create a pile of standing stones to commemorate a great event. Joshua had representatives of each tribe take a stone from the middle of the Jordan River which God miraculously caused to stop flowing. They put the stones on the other side of the river as an example to future generations of what God had done.

The standing stones were not just a visual for telling a story to future generations, they were a testament to the power, provision and faithfulness of God to the Israelites. We are to tell the same story today. The psalmist wrote in Psalm 145 that one generation is supposed to teach the next about the glorious splendor of God's majesty, about the power of His awesome works, and about His abundant goodness and righteousness.

We like to tell stories about great athletes and sports moments, but more important is telling others of what God has done for us. Think about what God has done in your life. What story do you have to tell? We can be standing stones – living testaments to others of God's power, mercy, and provision in our lives.

— PHILLIP BLOSSER, PH.D.

How do you share the truth? _____

_____

_____

_____

_____

_____

_____

_____

_____

_____

_____

_____

_____

THE WATERBOY

*" Everyone that drinks of this water will
be thirsty again, but whoever drinks of
the water that I will give him will never
be thirsty again. The water that I will
give him will become in him a spring
of water welling up to eternal life."*

JOHN 4:13-14 (ESV)

One of my favorite sports movies is The Waterboy starring Adam Sandler. If you would let me, I would like to draw a comparison of Sandler's character, Bobby Boucher, and Christ. Before you get all upset, track with me.

Even more today than ever before, coaches, athletes and parents are being taught the importance of good hydration and its benefits to performance. More and more drinks are being added to the market for hydration: Gatorade, G2, PowerAde, Vitamin Water, SmartWater, and the list goes on and on. Each of these drinks promises better hydration and better performance.

In the movie, this became the growing conflict because sports drinks were surpassing the desire for water. Boucher (Sandler) stuck to his convictions, though, and the superiority of plain water. He took it to a lowly team and raised them from "death" to glory.

In this comedy, and in sports, I see a great picture of Christ. When you look to the sidelines of any sport today, like in the movie, the coolers are full of Gatorade and its hefty promises. But when it comes down to it, those sports drinks are likely not better for us; they may actually be causing more damage with the sugar, sodium, and chemicals. And the truth is that most trainers and physicians will tell you nothing improves performance better than water.

We have to be hydrated in life as well; but are we drinking simple pure water from the well of Christ? Or have we been led to drink the sports drinks with empty promises of better performance and hydration only to be left cramping, bloated, and thirsty? What's in your water bottle?

— RYAN J. DiNUNZIO

What lies are you believing that cloud the truth? _____

_____

_____

_____

_____

_____

_____

_____

CAN I GET A MINUTE

"Let (no one) . . . say, 'The Lord will surely exclude me from his people.'"

ISAIAH 56:3

When I was a young teen, I spent countless hours collecting the autographs of baseball and hockey players. During summer afternoons, I could be found spending time in hotel lobbies waiting for baseball players to leave for the ballpark, or hanging around after games until they came out. All of the athletes were very nice about stopping. Likewise, hockey players were quite accommodating, signing my autograph book as I waited outside the arena after games. My efforts were rewarded as I have a vast collection of signatures from such superstars as Roberto Clemente, Willie Mays, Sandy Koufax, Bobby Orr, Bobby Hull, and Jean Beliveau.

Unfortunately, autograph seekers today have a much tougher time of trying to approach their heroes. Athletes are well-protected from the fans, either by hotel security, by fences around parking lots, or by departure buses parked inside the confines of stadiums.

While it's disappointing not to be able to get close to today's stars, no one ever has to worry about being shunned by the Lord. He is always available, in any situation and at any hour of the day, waiting and encouraging us to come to Him.

— LOIS THOMSON

How can you make better use of the Lord's accessibility? _____

_____

_____

_____

_____

_____

_____

_____

_____

_____

_____

_____

_____

_____

_____

119

"Never place a period where God has placed a comma. God is still speaking."
— Gracie Allen

"Remember Jesus Christ, raised from the dead, descended from David. This is my gospel, for which I am suffering even to the point of being chained like a criminal. But God's word is not chained."
— II Timothy 2:8-9

Scripture Index

Genesis
1:1, p. 92

Deuteronomy
32:4, p. 96

Joshua
1:5-8, p. 93

Judges
7:7, p. 87

I Samuel
17:32, p. 39
17:34-37, p. 47

II Chronicles
1:9-10, p. 84
31:21, p. 81

Esther
4:14, p. 66

Job
1:20-21, p. 70

Psalms
10:16, p. 113
27:14, p. 63
33:1, p. 24
34:9-11, p. 83
50:1-2, p. 44
73:26, p. 69
84:2, p. 41
111:7, p. 79
133:1-2, p. 17
145:3-7, p. 117

Proverbs
14:29-30, p. 60
16:26, p. 72
19:11, p. 21
19:20-22, p. 35
20:5, p. 26
27:17, p. 19

Ecclesiates
4:9-10, p. 7
5:10, p. 34

Isaiah
6:8, p. 50
56:3, p. 119

Matthew
5:41, p. 75
5:48, p. 99
12:25, p. 14
17:20, p. 89
23:12, p. 55
24:43-45, p. 45
26:74-75, p. 112

Mark
4:20, p. VIII
10:45, p. 59

Luke
1:37, p. 95
1:47-49, p. 48
6:27, p. 53
11:34, p. 11
12:48, p. 102
14:11, p. 58
14:28-30, p. 64
29:41-43, p. 46

John
1:12-13, p. 30
4:13-14, p. 118
8:32, p. 4
13:35, p. 116
14:6-7, p. 27
15:13, p. 54

Acts
12:5, p. 20
15:30-32 p. 9
17:28, p. 23
20:32, p. 82

Romans
5:3-5, p. 65
5:15, p. 108
8:35-37, p. 40
8:38-39, p. 62
12:1, p. 57
12:4-6, p. 15
14:7-8, p. 104

I Corinthians
3:12-13, p. 29
6:11, p. 111
6:14, p. 88
12:11, p. 42
13:1-3, p. 110
13:3-4, p. 56
15:31, p. 52
15:58, p. 78

II Corinthians
5:9, p. 32
5:11, p. 6
5:21, p. 105

Galatians
5:16-17, p. 5
5:22-23, p. 8
6:1, p. 94
6:4, p. 10

Ephesians
5:16, p. 28
6:18, p. VI

Philippians
1:6, p. 31
1:20, p. 103
2:1-4, p. 18
2:5-8, p. 86
2:15, p. 2
3:12, p. 77
3:14, p. 33
3:16, p. 100

Colossians
2:13-15, p. 114
2:14, p. 22
3:13, p. 115
3:23, p. 98

I Thessalonians
5:19, p. 74

II Timothy
2:8-9, p. 120
3:16-17, p. 51
4:1-2, p. 76
4:5-7, p. 80

Titus
1:7-8, p. 90
2:14, p. 16

Hebrews
3:13, p. 3
5:12, p. 68
7:11, p. 106
12:1-2, p. 67
12:12-14, p. 71

James
1:4, p. 101
3:6, p. 91

I Peter
1:13, p. 36
3:8, p. 12
3:15, p. 38
5:6-9, p. 43

I John
2:28, p. 107

TRAINING TABLE
CONTRIBUTORS

BILLY BARNARD
Billy Barnard is a freelance writer who has written several articles for *Sports Spectrum* magazine, and devotionals for *Training Table*.
P. 78

JASON BELCHER
Jason Belcher , an occasional writer for *Training Table*, works out of Charlotte, N.C., where he resides with his wife.
P. 14, 57, 69

PHILIP BLOSSER, PH.D
Philip Blosser, Ph.D is an associate professor at Liberty University. He has served in the marketing/promotions and ticketing sales areas and also received experience in sponsor and media relations while interning with Triple Crown Sports. He has also volunteered with Special Olympics and other local sporting events. Dr. Blosser currently resides in the Boonsboro, Va. area with his wife, and his three children.
P. 40, 117

CHRIS BOGGS
Chirs Boggs is the Director of Education at the Academy of Insurance at Insurance Journal and has written many devotionals for *Training Table* over the past two years. Chris currently resides just outside of the limits of Charlotte, N.C. in Union County.
P. 80, 91

TERRY BURWELL, RUNNING
Terry Burwell serves as the Principal at Champlain Discovery Public School in Ontario, Canada. In addition he is also very active in long disctance running competitively. He has been published several times in *Sports Spectrum* magazine.
P. 62

STEPHEN COPELAND, GOLF
Stephen Copeland is a member of the varsity golf team at Grace College in Indiana. He also works with the Grace College Sports Information Department and served as an intern for *Sports Spectrum*. Stephen has written several articles, features, and devotionals for the magazine as well.
P. 3, 5, 34, 88, 100, 115

JONATHAN CORRAO
Jonathan Corrao is an avid *Sports Spectrum* magazine reader; he had a "reader's submission" published in the Summer 2009 issue of *Training Table*.
P. 11

RYAN J. DINUNZIO, SOCCER

Ryan J. DiNunzio spent six years playing professional soccer in the United States. He also served with a missionary soccer team in Africa. Ryan has coached soccer at the collegiate and youth levels for more than 10 years. Currently he is the Vice President of Unlimited Success Sports Management, and the Core Media Group and is a contributing writer to *Sports Spectrum* magazine and *Training Table*. In addition, he is the Director of Operations for theGathering-Uptown. He resides in Charlotte, N.C. with his wife.

P. 2, 6, 10, 16, 21, 26, 30, 35, 38, 41, 42, 43, 44, 46, 65, 71, 79, 81, 83, 86, 90, 92, 95, 105, 118

TODD GREEN

Todd Green is an occasional writer for *Sports Spectrum* magazine, and *Training Table*; in addition he served as a youth pastor in Indiana.

P. 8, 66, 77

VICKIE GROOMS DENNY, PH.D, VOLLEYBALL

Coach Denny has 31 years of coaching experience on various levels of competition, and is the current coach of women's volleyball at Clearwater Christian College. She has contributed several devotionals to *Training Table*.

P. 18, 22

BRENDAN HANDEL

Brendan Handel is a freelance writer for *Sports Spectrum* magazine, and *Training Table*. Brendan lives in Charlotte, N.C.

P. 51

BRETT HONEYCUTT, RUNNING

Brett Honeycutt is the Managing Editor of *Sports Spectrum* magazine. He is a consistent contributor to the magazine and devotional. Before coming to Sports Spectrum, Brett worked as a sports writer for the Charlotte Observer. He ran track and cross country at Liberty University. Currently he is the cross country and track coach at Metrolina Christian Academy. He resides with his wife in Huntersville, N.C.

P. 9, 29, 31, 50, 52, 58, 63, 67, 68, 70, 82, 93, 110, 112, 116

PAUL KELLY

Paul Kelly is an avid reader *Sports Spectrum* magazine and *Training Table*. He has had several "reader submissions" published in various issues of *Training Table*.

P. 27

LEAH METCALF, BASKETBALL

Leah Metcalf is a former member of the University of Nort Carolina Chapel Hill women's basketball team. Currenlty she plays professional basketball in France. She has spent time in Germany as well during her career. Leah has been a contributing writer to *Training Table*.

P. 101, 106

ALAN MORGAN

Alan Morgan is a freelance writer for *Training Table*. He lives in Charlotte, N.C.

P. 87

DAVID NOELL
David Noell worked as an intern for *Sports Spectrum* magazine. During his time with the company he contributed several devotionals for *Training Table*, and wrote an article for the magazine. He also worked as an Assistant to the Editor and wrote several short testimonies of athletes for posting on www.sportsspectrum.com. David is a graduate of the Medill School of Journalism and works as a freelance sports writer in Chicago.
P. 55, 64, 104

BRIAN PAYNE
Brian Payne has contributed several devotionals for *Training Table*. Brian worked as an intern for Sports Spectrum on the Power To Win vidoes in 2008 and 2009. He resides in Charlotte, N.C. with his wife.
P. 47

JEFF PINKLETON
Jeff Pinkleton is a contributing writer to *Training Table*. He lives in Springfield, Ohio. Jeff is the City Director for The Gathering Springfield, a men's discipleship/ ministry program.
P. 89, 99

AARON POLSGROVE
Aaron Polsgrove is the Assistant to the Chairman and CEO at Coca-Cola Consolidated in Charlotte, N.C.. A graduate of West Point Military Academy, Aaron served this country for six years before taking his post with Coca-Cola. He currenlty lives in Charlotte with his wife and children.
P. 19, 54

TIM SEARS
Tim Sears is a freelance writer who has written for *Training Table*. Tim currently resides in Kansas City, Mo.
P. 74

BURNEY SHEALEY
Burney Shealey is a lay pastor in Framingham, Massachusetts, where he lives with his wife. Burney has contributed several devotionals to *Training Table*.
P. 23

LEAH SHAIKH
Leah Shaikh works full-time for Athletes in Action at the University of South Floirda with her husband Asif.
P. 103

MARK STEFFENS, SOCCER
Mark Steffens is the coach of the Charlotte Eagles, a professional missionary soccer team. Mark has led the Eagles to the USL-2 Championship match seven times, and has won the championship in 2000 and 2005. The United Soccer Leagues recognized Steffens for his amazing record and commitment to the community in 2007 as he was inducted into the USL Hall of Fame. Mark and his wife have three daughters, and nine grandchildren. They currently reside in Waxhaw, N.C.
P. 98

STEVEN STINSON
Steven Stinson is the Pastor of Recreation at Northside Baptist in Charlotte, N.C. Steven has been a contributing wrtier for *Training Table*.
P. 94, 114

JEAN-RENE TASSY
Jean-Rene Tassy is the Ministry Director at the Alliance Academy in Quito, Ecuador. Jean-Rene is a graduate of Messiah College and has worked in youth, family, and sports ministry for more than 15 years. He lives in Quito with his wife and three children.
P. 32

LOIS THOMSON
Lois Thomson, an occasional writer for *Sports Spectrum* magazine and *Training Table*, works out of Pittsburgh, Pa.
P. 59, 119

COREY THOMPSON
Corey Thompson is a freelance writer and public school teacher in Charlotte, N.C. who has written for *Training Table* on several occasions. Corey currently resides in Charlotte.
P. 15, 102

ALAN TYSON, SPORTS MEDICINE
Alan Tyson is the President of Architech Sports and Physical Therapy. He was the former Vice President of Sports Performance and Rehabilitation for OrthoCarolina. He also works with the Charlotte Knights (AAA affiliate of the Chicago White Sox), the Carolina Panthers and Charlotte Eagles as a consultant. Alan has authored three books for the female athlete, the baseball pitcher, and for football players preparing for the NFL combines. Alan is also an associate editor of the National Strength and Conditioning Journal.
P. 7

KRYSTIL WADE
Krystil Wade has done work for *Sports Spectrum* as a copy editor on occasion. Krystil is a middle school English teacher and resides in Charlotte, N.C.
P. 107

NATHAN WADE
Nathan Wade is the Director of Marketing and Adverstising for *Sports Spectrum*. He also has been a contributing writer to *Training Table*, and manages the magazine's social media and networks.
P. 17, 20, 42, 56

ROBERT WALKER
Robert Walker earned a B.S. in Physical Education, and a Masters Degree in Sports Management. He has served on the boards for both Fellowship of Christian Athletes (FCA) and Sports Outreach America (SOA). He also spent a considerable amount of time coaching basketball, soccer, and baseball at two different Christian schools. Robert is currently the President and CEO of Unlimited Success Sports Management and The Core Media Group. Robert is the Publisher of *Sports Spectrum* magazine and *Training Table*. He currently resides in North Carolina with his wife and two children.
P. 4, 33, 39, 45, 59

Jeff Weaver

Jeff Weaver is an avid *Sports Spectrum* magazine reader. He had a "reader submission" published in the Summer 2010 issue of *Training Table*.
P. 113

BT West, III

BT West is a committed reader of *Sports Spectrum* magazine and *Training Table*. BT had a "reader's submission" published in the Spring 2010 issue of *Training Table*.
P. 53

John Zeller

John Zeller is the Executive Vice President of Score International. He has been an occasional contributor to *Training Table*. He lives in Zephyrhills, Fla. with his wife and children.
P. 28, 75, 76

Stephanie Zonars

Stephanie Zonars is a freelance writer who has written varios articles for *Sports Spectrum* magazine as well as the "Coaching Zone" feature. She is the author of *Leader of the Pack: The Legacy of Legendary Coach Kay Yow* (2009), and *Timeout: Moments with God for Winning in Life* (2008).
P. 111

OTHER GREAT PRODUCTS FROM -

PERIODICALS

Sports Spectrum

Sports Spectrum magazine seeks to highlight Christian athletes of all sports and levels to help motivate, encourage and inspire people in their faith through the exciting and challenging world of sports.

Training Table

Training Table is a place to go and indulge in the Bread of Life while God stretches your soul. Three months of daily sports-related devotionals. 4 issues: Fall, Winter, Spring and Summer.

DVDS & VIDEOS

Power To Win

Power To Win is a high-impact, 20-minute DVD presentation featuring current NFL players. It provides a gripping story and testimony and a clear explanation of the plan of salvation. It is evangelicalistic and powerful outreach tool.

FOR MORE INFORMATION VISIT OUR STORE AT:
WWW.SPORTSSPECTRUM.COM

Silver Anniversary Edition:
Celebrating 25 Years of Sports & Faith

An inspiring book that tells the faith stories of the 25 most impactful Christian sports figures who've appeared in *Sports Spectrum* magazine the last 25 years. Like the magazine, these stories will inspire you in your faith or cause you to examine your life to see if Christ is a part of it.

Drive Thru Succes:
Finding Success While Waiting in the Drive Thru

Looking to live a successful life? Then take a seat and join the ride in *Drive Thru Success*, by Robert B. Walker - a successful pro sports agent for more than 20 years who uses the drive thru experience as an illustration for finding true success in life. Each step of the drive thru experience represents a different step for success. *Drive Thru Success* is a great read for everyone of any age who is searching to achieve success in business, athletics, school, and life.

Life Points:
25 Directives That Will Change the Way You Live

Whether you're a businessperson, parent, student, or athlete, life can be confusing. If you don't have the information you want, it can be frustrating. But if you don't have the direction you need, it can be devastating. *Life Points*, by Dr. Steve Jirgal, has been written to add the directives needed to set your life on a course of success. By systematically following the book's directives, you will have the motivation, information, and plans to accomplish so much more in your life.

Cultivating the Godly Athlete:
Our Faith On and Off the Field

Ryan J. DiNunzio discusses 20 biblical qualities, highlighted by Paul, for the spiritual development of athletes on and off the field. This is an in-depth look at what faith on the field looks like, and how our lives as Christians are to mirror in our endeavors, including sports.

COMING
2011

Living the Thankful Life

COMING
2011

Another title by Robert B. Walker, he discusses what it looks like to live life in a truly thankful manner. Based on I Thessalonians 5:18, *Living the Thankful Life* guides you in your quest to always be thankful. It includes 30 short stories from Robert's life along with scripture and space to write notes.

CPSIA information can be obtained at www.ICGtesting.com
Printed in the USA
BVOW030143050112

279646BV00004B/3/P